外国人镜头中的八国联军

—— 辛丑条约百年图志

The Eight-Power Allied Forces Through Foreigners' Camera

An Illustrated Record of the *Protocol of 1901*

1900—1901

中国人权发展基金会
中国第一历史档案馆 编

China Foundation for
Human Rights Development
The First Historical Archives of China

前　言

2001年9月7日，对于中国乃至一些发达国家都是一个具有特殊意义的日子。整整一个世纪前即1901年的今天，英、美、法、德、日、俄、奥、意等八国组成侵华联军，强迫清政府签订了人类文明史上最蛮横、最不平等的条约，此年为中国辛丑年，史称辛丑条约。本图册以照片真实反映了这一段历史。

这些照片主要是外国人拍摄的。其中三分之一第一次面世，拍摄者是一位亲身参与联军侵华的英国军人。1996年英籍华人陈钧先生在英国伦敦佳士德拍卖行购得这些照片，遂转赠予中国第一历史档案馆。这些百年前的镜头，给人以历史的启示和教益。

在八国联军炮击和烧杀抢掠下，京津一带几十座城镇和几百个村庄成为废墟，北京城内断壁残垣四处可见；奋起反抗的义和团民、清军官兵和无辜百姓惨遭杀戮，尸首遍地；皇家珍宝及科学仪器被抢，商贾富户财产遭劫，连喇嘛寺庙的财物也被掠夺；数不清的百姓衣不遮体，无家可归……这些照片真实地记录了战争给中国人民造成的极大创伤。

八国联军威逼年收入仅有8000万两白银的清政府，赔偿列强白银4.5亿两，39年还清本息，总计9.8亿两。巨额赔款，国库亏空，人民遭受重重压迫，积贫积弱的中国进一步走向灾难深渊。照片令人深思，每一个国家的发展都有一个积累和渐进的过程，不少发展中国家都曾遭受列强掠夺与摧残，各国经济联系更加紧密的今天，发达国家有责任支持发展中国家尽快发展。

八国联军威逼清政府解除京、津、唐战略要地武装，允由列强驻兵，镇压人民反抗，重惩附和义和团的官吏，承认列强在北京扩大使馆区和永久驻军，允许其在华享有广泛领事裁判、协定关税、海关控制、沿海贸易、江河航行、开矿筑路、租界等权利。偌大中国几无主权可言，中国人民遭受列强任意欺侮和杀戮，无人权可述。从照片反映的史实清楚看出，失去了国家主权，人权就是梦想。

中国和世界人民渴望所有国家相互尊重主权和人权，共同发展和繁荣。世界要和平，人民要合作，国家要发展，社会要进步，是任何势力都无法逆转的时代潮流。这是本图册给我们的历史性启示。

Preface

September 7, 2001 marks a special day for China and even some developed countries. On this day one century ago, namely, September 7, 1901, the Eight-Power Allied Forces formed by Britain, the United States, France, Germany, Japan, Russia, Austria and Italy forced the Qing Government to sign the most insolent and unequal treaty in human civilization. That year was the Year of Xinchou in Chinese lunar calendar, so the treaty, officially the *Protocol of 1901*, is historically known as the *Treaty of Xinchou*. Photos in this illustrated book present a true picture of this period of history.

These photos were mainly taken by foreigners. One-third of them, which are made public for the first time, were taken by a British officer who personally participated in the invasion of China as a member of the Allied Forces. Mr. Chen Jun, a Chinese Britishman, bought these photos from Christie's in London in 1996 and later on donated them to the First Historical Archives of China. Readers will gain historical enlightenment from these photos taken 100 years ago.

Under the shelling of the Eight-Power Allied Forces and the subsequent burning, killing and pillaging, dozens of towns and hundreds of villages in the areas of Beijing and Tianjin were reduced to rubble. Everywhere in the City of Beijing was crumbling walls and ruined curbs. The Boxers rising up in resistance, the officers and soldiers in the Qing government forces and innocent Chinese were massacred in cold blood. Royal treasures and scientific instruments, property of business firms and wealthy families, and even property of lama temples were plundered. Countless Chinese became homeless, having insufficient clothing to cover their nakedness. These photos are authentic records of the extremely miserable life of the Chinese people as a result of the war.

The Eight-Power Allied Forces forced the Qing Government, which had only 80 million taels of silver in annual revenue, to pay an indemnity of 450 million taels of silver to the powers. The principal and interest of the indemnity, which were scheduled to pay off in 39 years, totaled 980 million taels of silver. As a consequence of the huge amount of indemnities and the heavy government deficits, the people suffered all kinds of oppression. The poor and weak China went further in the abyss of misery. The photos are thought provoking—the development of every country has a process of accumulation and progressive advancement, and many developing countries had suffered the plunder and trample of the strong powers. Today, as economic ties among various countries have become increasingly close, developed countries have the obligation to support the developing countries.

The Eight-Power Allied Forces forced the Qing Government to disarm strategically important areas in Beijing, Tianjin and Tangshan, permit garrisons by the powers, suppress the people's resistance, severely punish officials supporting the Boxers, allow the powers to expand the legation quarters in Beijing and garrison troops permanently, allow them to enjoy extensive consular jurisdiction in China as well as rights for tariff agreement, Customs control, coastal trade, river navigation, mining and railway construction, concession, etc. China, in spite of its big size, had little sovereignty left. Chinese people were subject to the bullying and killing by the powers, and no human rights whatever could be spoken of. Historical facts reflected by the photos clearly reveal that human rights are nothing but an illusion without national sovereignty.

People in China and the rest of the world long for mutual respect to sovereignty, human rights, common development and prosperity. The world needs peace and people want cooperation. Every nation needs development and every society wants to make progress. This is a trend of the times that no force can reverse. This is also the historical enlightenment shed by this illustrated book.

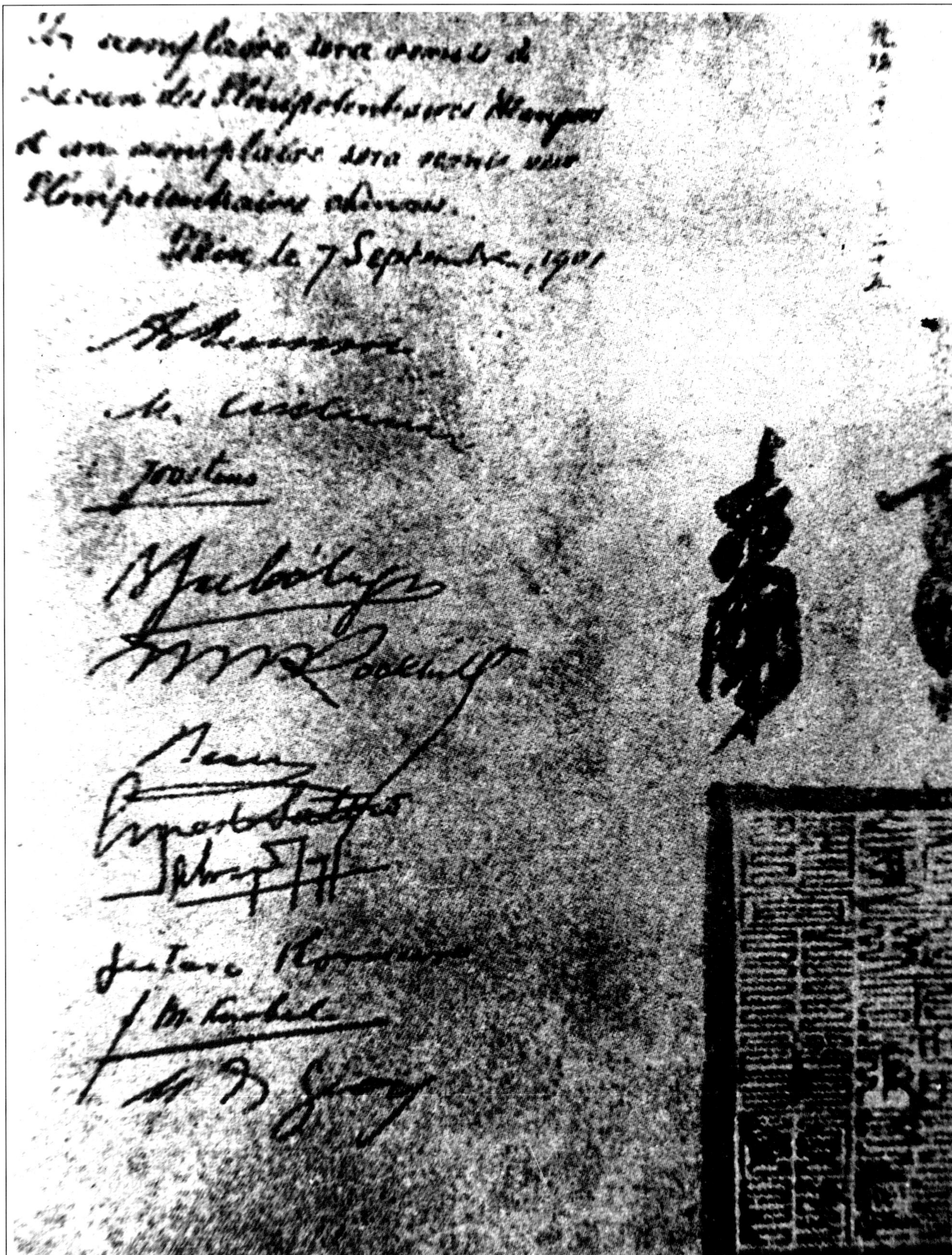

Un exemplaire sera remis à chacun des Plénipotentiaires Étrangers et un exemplaire sera remis aux Plénipotentiaires Chinois.

Pékin, le 7 Septembre, 1901

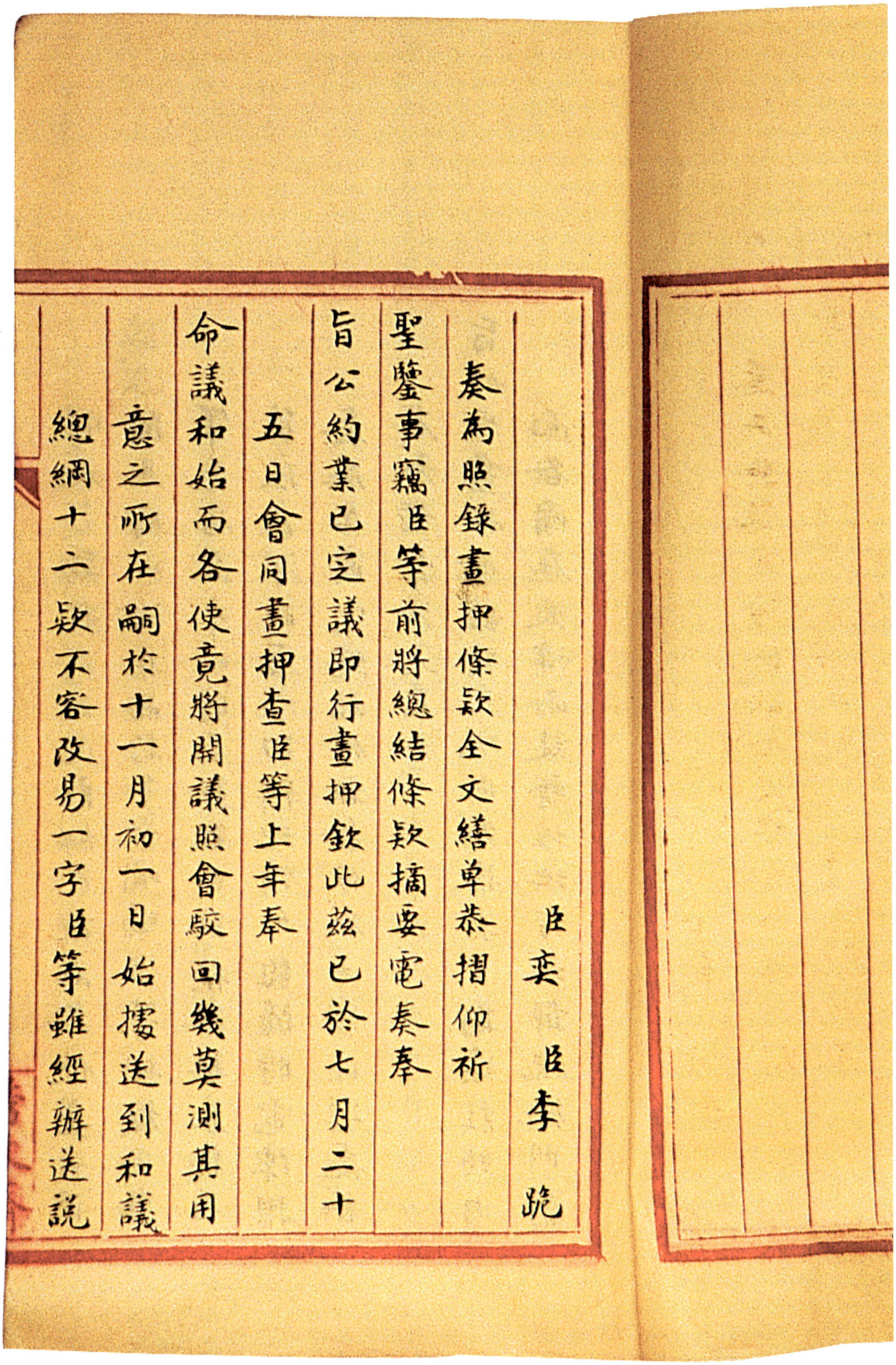

臣奕　臣李　跪

奏為照錄畫押條款全文繕單恭摺仰祈

聖鑒事竊臣等前將總結條款摘要電奏奉

旨公約業已定議即行畫押欽此茲已於七月二十

五日會同畫押查臣等上年奉

命議和始而各使竟將開議照會駁回幾莫測其用

意之所在嗣於十一月初一日始據送到和議

總綱十二款不容改易一字臣等雖經辦送說

《辛丑条约》条款全录。　1

The full text of the *Protocol of 1901*

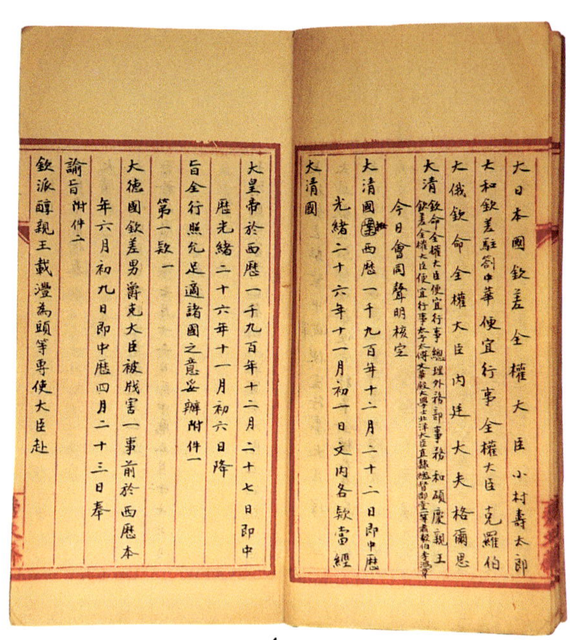

大日本國欽差全權大臣小村壽太郎
大和欽差駐劄中華便宜行事全權大臣克羅伯
大俄欽命全權大臣內廷大夫格爾思
大清欽命全權大臣便宜行事總理外務部事務和碩慶親王
欽差全權大臣便宜行事太子太傅文華殿大學士北洋大臣直隸總督部堂一等肅毅伯李鴻章
今日會同聲明核定
大清國暨西歷一千九百年十二月二十二日即中歷
光緒二十六年十一月初一日文內各款當經
大清國

大皇帝於西歷一千九百年十二月二十七日即中
歷光緒二十六年十一月初六日降
旨全行照允足適諸國之意妥辦附件一
第一款一
大德國欽差男爵克大臣被戕害一事前於西歷本
年六月初九日即中歷四月二十三日奉
諭旨附件二
欽派醇親王載灃為頭等專使大臣赴

4

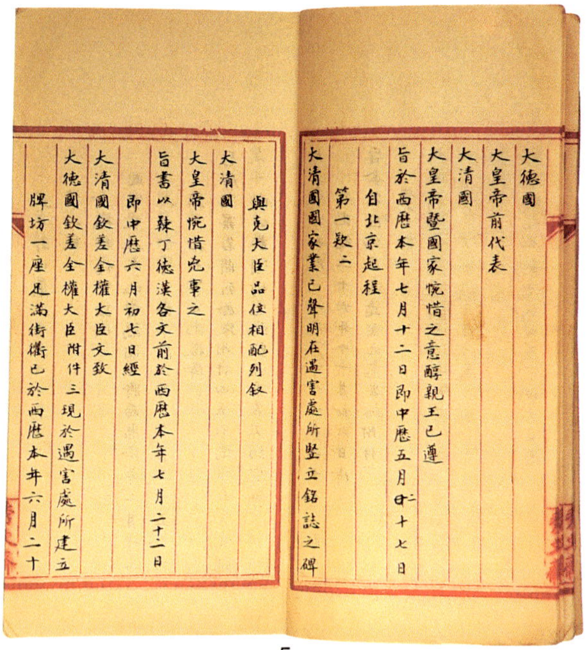

大德國
大皇帝前代表
大清國
大皇帝暨國家惋惜之意醇親王已遵
旨於西歷本年七月十二日即中歷五月廿二十七日
自北京起程
第一款二
大清國國家業已聲明在遇害處所豎立銘誌之碑

與克大臣品位相配列叙
大清國
大皇帝惋惜兇事之
旨書以辣丁德漢各文前於西歷本年七月二十二日
即中歷六月初七日經
大清國欽差全權大臣文致
大德國欽差全權大臣附件三現於遇害處所建立
牌坊一座足滿街衢已於西歷本年六月二十

5

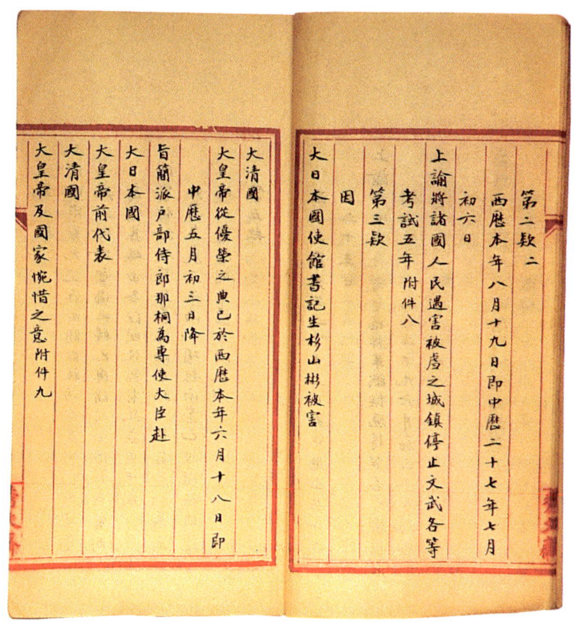

第二款二
西歷本年八月十九日即中歷二十七年七月
初六日
上諭將諸國人民遇害被虐之城鎮停止文武各等
考試五年附件八
第三款
因
大日本國使館書記生杉山彬被害

大清國
大皇帝從優榮之典已於西歷本年六月十八日即
中歷五月初三日降
旨簡派戶部侍郎那桐為專使大臣赴
大日本國
大皇帝前代表
大清國
大皇帝及國家惋惜之意附件九

8

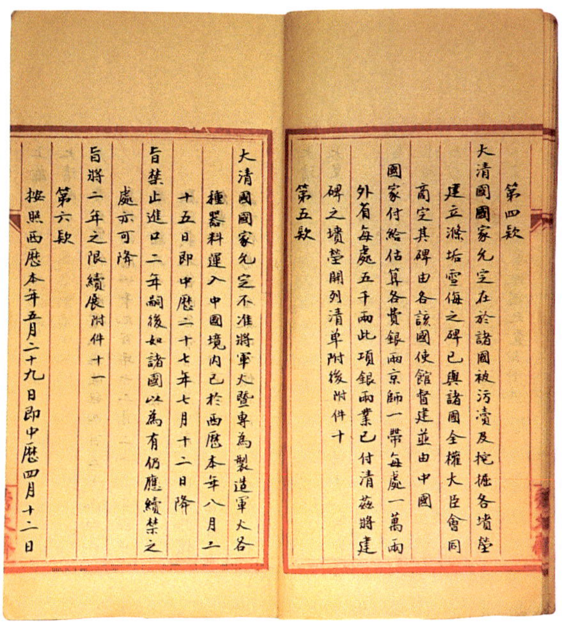

第四款
大清國國家允定在於諸國被污瀆及挖掘各墳塋
建立滌垢雪侮之碑已與諸國全權大臣會同
商定其碑由各該國使館督建並由中國
國家付給估算各費銀兩京師一帶每處一萬兩
外省每處五千兩此項銀兩業已付清茲將建
碑之墳塋開列清單附後附件十
第五款

大清國國家允定不准將軍火暨專為製造軍火各
種器料運入中國境內已於西歷本年八月二
十五日即中歷二十七年七月十二日降
旨禁止進口二年嗣後如諸國以為有仍應續禁之
處亦可降
旨將二年之限續展附件十一
第六款
按照西歷本年五月二十九日即中歷四月十二日

9

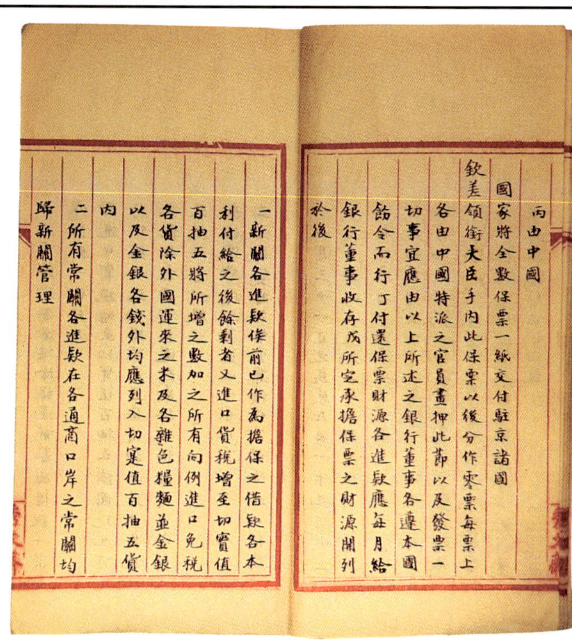

丙由中國
國家將全數保票一紙交付駐京諸國
欽差領銜大臣手內此保票以後分作零票每票上
各由中國特派之官員畫押此節以及發票一
切事宜應由以上所述之銀行董事各遵本國
飭令而行丁付還保票財源各進款應每月給
銀行董事收存戊所定承擔保票之財源開列
於後

一新關各進款俟前已作為擔保之借款各本
利付給之後餘剩者又進口貨稅增至切實值
百抽五將所增之數加之所有向例進口免稅
各貨除外國運來之米及各雜色糧麵並金銀
以及金銀各錢外均應列入切實值百抽五貨
內
二所有常關各進款在各通商口岸之常關均
歸新關管理

12

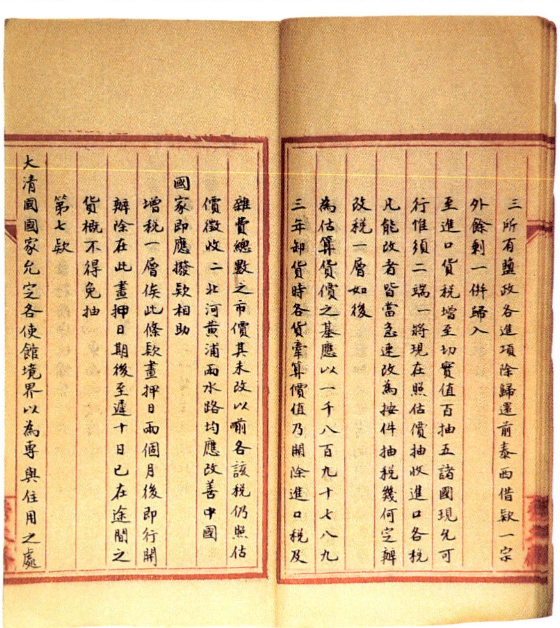

三所有鹽政各進項除歸還前泰西借款一宗
外餘剩一併歸入
至進口貨稅增至切實值百抽五諸國現允可
行惟須二端一將現在照估價抽收進口各稅
凡能改者皆當急速改為按件抽稅幾何定辦
改稅一層如後
為估算貨價之基應以一千八百九十七八九
三年卸貨時各貨牽算價值乃開除進口稅及

雜費總數之市價其未改以前各該稅仍照估
價徵收二北河黃浦兩水路均應改善中國
國家即應撥款相助
增稅一層俟此條款畫押日兩個月後即行開
辦除在此畫押日期後至遲十日已在途間之
貨概不得免抽
第七款
大清國國家允定各使館境界以為專與住用之處

13

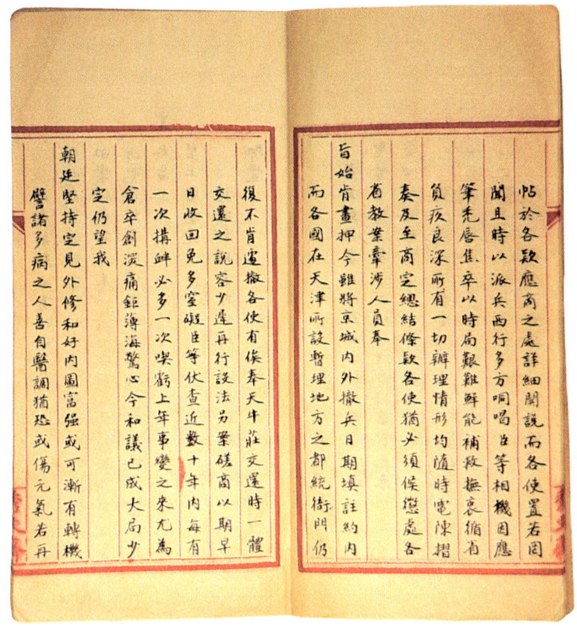

帖於各款應商之處詳細聞說而各使置若罔
聞且時以派兵西行多方恫喝臣等相機因應
筆舌唇焦卒以時局艱難鮮能補救撫衷循省
負疚良深所有一切辦理情形均隨時電陳摺
奏及至商定總結條款各使猶必須候懲處各
省教案牽涉人員奉
旨始肯畫押今雖將京城內外撤兵日期填註約內
而各國在天津所設暫理地方之都統衙門仍
復不肯遽撤各使有俟奉天牛莊交還時一體
交還之說容少遲再行設法另案磋商以期早
日收回免多窒礙臣等伏查近數十年內每有
一次搆衅必多一次喫虧上年事變之來尤為
倉卒創深痛鉅薄海驚心今和議已成大局少
定仍望我
朝廷堅持定見外修和好內圖富強或可漸有轉機
譬諸多病之人善自醫調猶恐或傷元氣若再

2

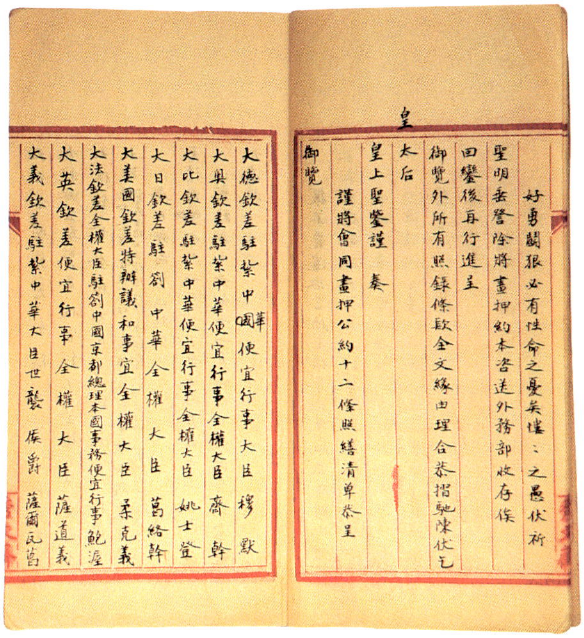

好勇鬬狠必有性命之憂矣懔懔之愚伏祈
聖明垂鑒除將畫押約本咨送外務部收存俟
回鑾後再行進呈
御覽外所有照錄條款全文緣由理合恭摺馳陳伏乞
皇太后
皇上聖鑒謹奏
謹將會同畫押公約十二條照繕清單恭呈
御覽
大德欽差駐紮中華便宜行事大臣穆默
大奥欽差駐紮中華便宜行事全權大臣齊幹
大比欽差駐紮中華便宜行事全權大臣姚士登
大日欽差駐劄中華全權大臣葛絡幹
大美國欽差特辦議和事宜全權大臣柔克義
大法欽差全權大臣駐劄中國京都總理本國事務便宜行事鮑渥
大英欽差便宜行事全權大臣薩道義
大義欽差駐紮中華大臣世襲侯爵薩爾瓦葛

3

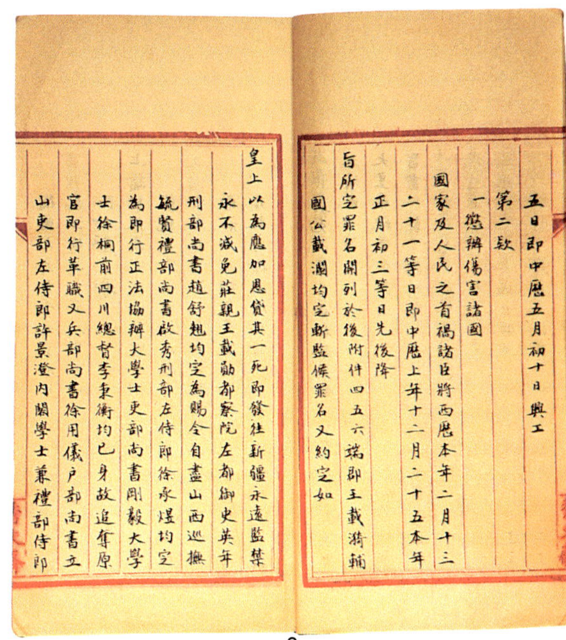

五日即中歷五月初十日興工
第二款
一懲辦傷害諸國
國家及人民之首禍諸臣將西歷本年二月十三
二十一等日即中歷上年十二月二十五本年
正月初三等日先後降
旨所定罪名開列於後附件四五六端郡王載漪輔
國公載瀾均定斬監候罪名又約定如
皇上以為應加恩貸其一死即發往新疆永遠監禁
永不減免莊親王載勛都察院左都御史英年
刑部尚書趙舒翹均定為賜令自盡山西巡撫
毓賢禮部尚書啟秀刑部左侍郎徐承煜均定
為即行正法協辦大學士吏部尚書剛毅大學
士徐桐前四川總督李秉衡均已身故追奪原
官即行革職又兵部尚書徐用儀戶部尚書立
山吏部左侍郎許景澄內閣學士兼禮部侍郎

6

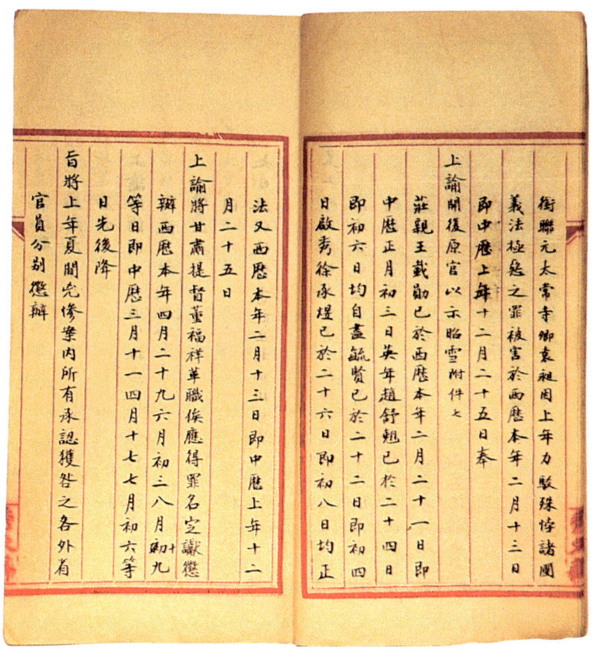

銜聯元太常寺卿袁昶因上年力駁殊悖諸國
義法極惡之罪被害於西歷本年二月十三日
即中歷上年十二月二十五日奉
上諭開復原官以示昭雪附件七
莊親王載勛已於西歷本年二月二十一日即
中歷正月初三日英年趙舒翹已於二十四日
即初六日均自盡毓賢已於二十二日即初四
日啟秀徐承煜已於二十六日即初八日均正
法又西歷本年二月十三日即中歷上年十二
月二十五日
上諭將甘肅提督董福祥革職俟應得罪名定讞懲
辦西歷本年四月二十九六月初三八月初十九
等日即中歷三月十一四月十七七月初六等
日先後降
旨將上年夏間兇慘案內所有承認獲咎之各外省
官員分別懲辦

7

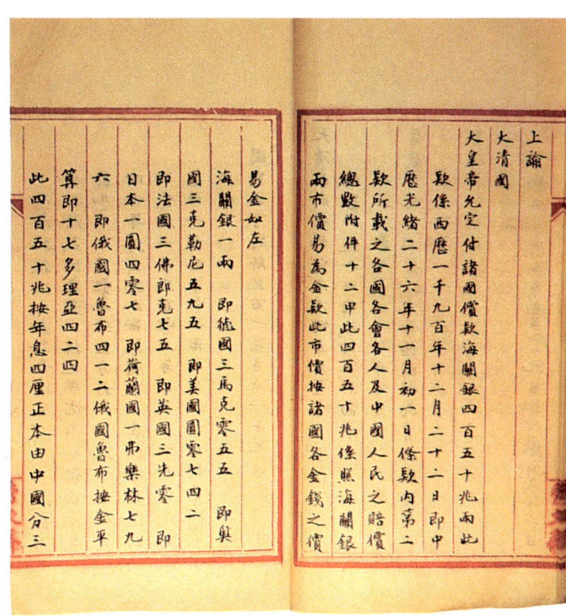

上諭
大清國
大皇帝允定付諸國償款海關銀四百五十兆兩此
款係西歷一千九百年十二月二十二日即中
歷光緒二十六年十一月初一日條款內第二
款所載之各國各會各人及中國人民之賠償
總數附件十二中此四百五十兆係照海關銀
兩市價易為金款此市價按諸國各金錢之價
易金如左
海關銀一兩　即德國三馬克零五五　即奧
國三克勒尼五九五　即美國圜零七四二
即法國三佛郎克七五　即英國三先零　即
日本一圓四零七　即荷蘭國一弗樂林七九
六　即俄國一魯布四一二俄國魯布按金平
算即十七多理亞四二四
此四百五十兆按年息四釐正本由中國分三

10

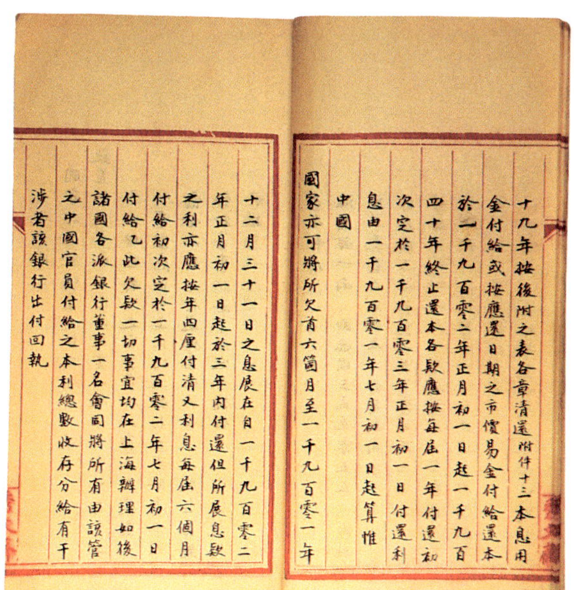

十九年按後附之表各章清還附件十三本息用
金付給或按應還日期之市價易金付給還本
於一千九百零二年正月初一日起一千九百
四十年終止還本各款應按每屆一年付還初
次定於一千九百零三年正月初一日付還利
息由一千九百零一年七月初一日起算惟
中國
國家亦可將所欠首六箇月至一千九百零一年
十二月三十一日之息展在自一千九百零二
年正月初一日起於三年內付還但所展息款
之利亦應按年四釐付清又利息每屆六個月
付給初次定於一千九百零二年七月初一日
付給乙此欠款一切事宜均在上海辦理如後
諸國各派銀行董事一名會同將所有由該管
之中國官員付給之本利總數收存分給有干
涉者該銀行出付回執

11

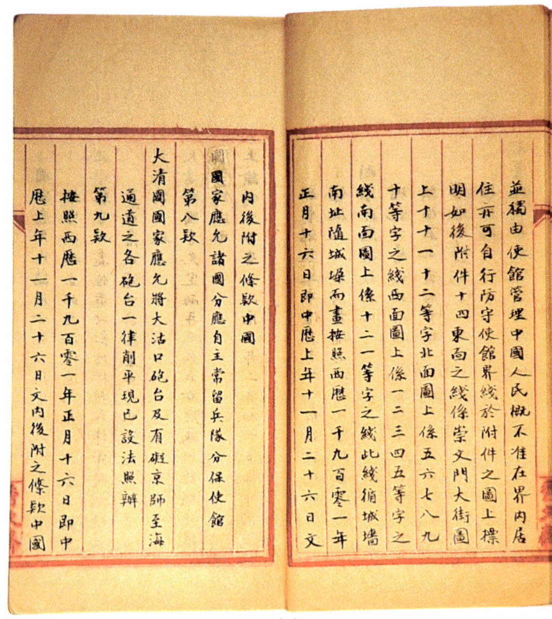

並獨由使館管理中國人民概不准在界內居
住亦可自行防守使館界綫於附件之圖上標
明如後附件十四東面之綫係崇文門大街圖
上十十一十二等字北面圖上係五六七八九
十等字之綫西面圖上係一二三四五等字之
綫南面圖上係十二一等字之綫此綫循城墻
南址隨城堞而畫按照西歷一千九百零一年
正月十六日即中歷上年十一月二十六日文
內後附之條款中國
國家應允諸國分應自主常留兵隊分保使館
第八款
大清國國家應允將大沽口砲台及有礙京師至海
通道之各砲台一律削平現已設法照辦
第九款
按照西歷一千九百零一年正月十六日即中
歷上年十一月二十六日文內後附之條款中國

14

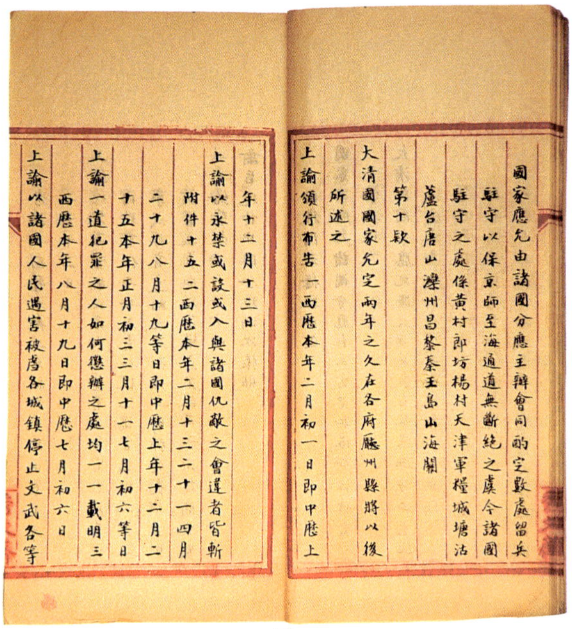

國家應允由諸國分應主辦會同酌定數處留兵
駐守以保京師至海通道無斷絕之虞今諸國
駐守之處係黃村郎坊楊村天津軍糧城塘沽
蘆台唐山灤州昌黎秦王島山海關
第十款
大清國國家允定兩年之久在各府廳州縣將以後
所述之
上諭頒行布告一西歷本年二月初一日即中歷上
年十二月十三日
上諭以永禁或設或入與諸國仇敵之會違者皆斬
附件十五二西歷本年二月十三二十一四月
二十九八月十九等日即中歷本年十二月二
十五本年正月初三三月十一七月初六等日
上諭一道犯罪之人如何懲辦之處均一一載明三
西歷本年八月十九日即中歷七月初六日
上諭以諸國人民遇害被虐各城鎮停止文武各等

15

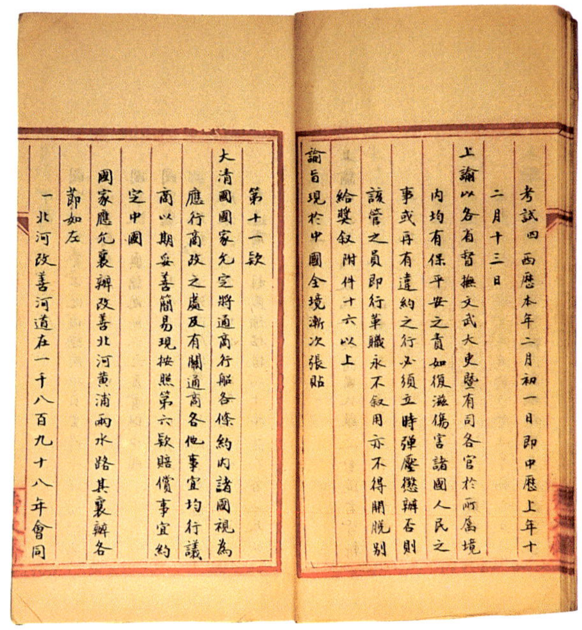

考試四西歷本年二月初一日即中歷上年十
二月十三日
上諭以各省督撫文武大吏暨有司各官於所屬境
內均有保平安之責如復滋傷害諸國人民之
事或再有違約之行必須立時彈壓懲辦否則
該管之員即行革職永不叙用亦不得開脫別
給獎叙附件十六以上
諭旨現於中國全境漸次張貼
第十一款
大清國國家允定將通商行船各條約內諸國視為
應行商改之處及有關通商各他事宜均行議
商以期妥善簡易現按照第六款賠償事宜約
定中國
國家應允襄辦改善北河黃浦兩水路其襄辦各
節如左
一北河改善河道在一千八百九十八年會同

16

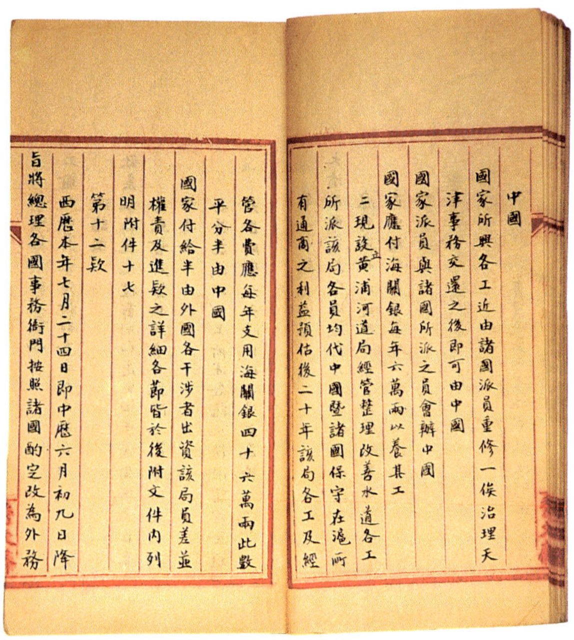

中國
國家所興各工近由諸國派員重修一俟治理天
津事務交還之後即可由中國
國家派員與諸國所派之員會辦中國
國家應付海關銀每年六萬兩以養其工
二現設立黃浦河道局經管整理改善水道各工
所派該局各員均代中國暨諸國保守在滬所
有通商之利益預估後二十年該局各工及經
管各費應每年支用海關銀四十六萬兩此數
平分半由中國
國家付給半由外國各干涉者出資該局員差並
權責及進款之詳細各節皆於後附文件內列
明附件十七
第十二款
西歷本年七月二十四日即中歷六月初九日降
旨將總理各國事務衙門按照諸國酌定改為外務

17

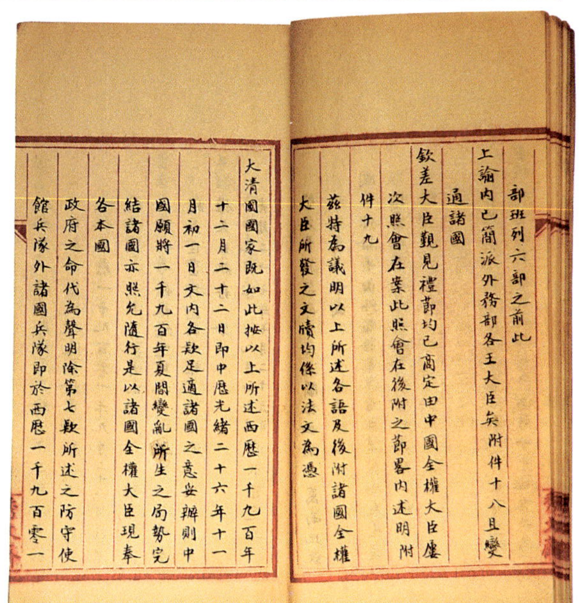

部班列六部之前此
上諭內已簡派外務部各王大臣矣附件十八且變
通諸國
欽差大臣覲見禮節均已商定由中國全權大臣屢
次照會在案此照會在後附之節畧內述明附
件十九
茲特為議明以上所述各語及後附諸國全權
大臣所發之文牘均係以法文為憑
大清國國家既如此按以上所述西歷一千九百年
十二月二十二日即中歷光緒二十六年十一
月初一日文內各款足適諸國之意妥辦則中
國願將一千九百年夏間變亂所生之局勢完
結諸國亦照允隨行是以諸國全權大臣現奉
各本國
政府之命代為聲明除第七款所述之防守使
館兵隊外諸國兵隊即於西歷一千九百零一

18

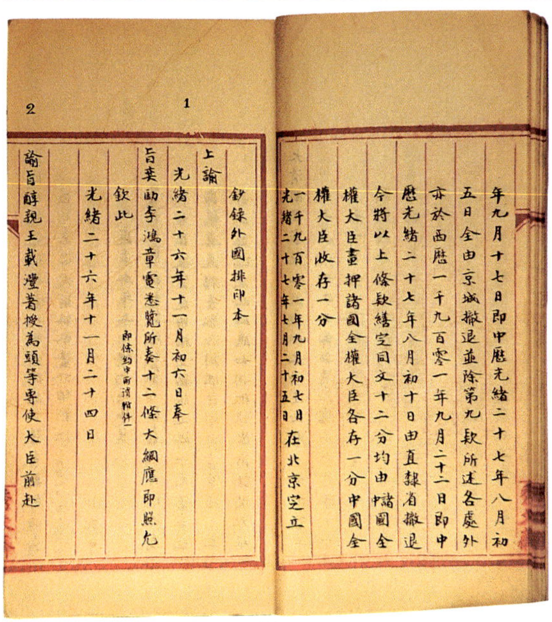

年九月十七日即中歷光緒二十七年八月初
五日全由京城撤退並除第九款所述各處外
亦於西歷一千九百零一年九月二十二日即中
歷光緒二十七年八月初十日由直隸省撤退
今將以上條款繕定同文十二分均由諸國全
權大臣畫押諸國全權大臣各存一分中國全
權大臣收存一分
一千九百零一年九月初七日
光緒二十七年七月二十五日 在北京定立

1

鈔錄外國排印本
上諭
光緒二十六年十一月初六日奉
旨奕劻李鴻章電奏覽所奏十二條大綱應即照允
欽此（即條約中所謂附件一）
光緒二十六年十一月二十四日

2

諭旨醇親王載灃著授為頭等專使大臣前赴

19

目 录 CONTENTS

八国联军入侵前的中国

China Before the Invasion of the Eight-Power Allied Forces

19世纪30年代，英国向中国大规模走私鸦片，在政治、经济、社会等诸多方面给中国带来严重危害。清政府痛下决心，派湖广总督林则徐赴广东禁烟。

1840年，英国向中国不宣而战。中国沿海及长江沿岸的舟山、宁波、吴淞、镇江等城镇相继遭到英国舰炮轰袭。1842年8月，清政府被迫签订了中国近代史上第一个不平等条约——中英《南京条约》。尔后的60年里，清政府国门洞开。中美《望厦条约》、中法《黄埔条约》、中俄《瑷珲条约》、中日《马关条约》……一系列不平等条约接连不断，割地、赔款、驻军、自由传教、鸦片贸易公开等等，丧权辱国，日甚一日。殖民主义强国掌握了中国的海关管理权、关税协定权…… 享有领事裁判权、发行钞票权等等，蚕食鲸吞中国主权。中国人痛恨不平等条约，义和团起事喊出："最恨和约，误国殃民，上行下效，民冤不伸"。

In the 1830s, Britain illegally imported opium to China in large quantities, bringing severe damage to China in political, economic, social and other aspects. The Qing Government finally made a resolute decision and dispatched Lin Zexu, Governor-General of Hubei and Hunan, to ban opium smoking and the opium trade in Guangdong.

In 1840, Britain launched an undeclared war on China. Cities and towns along Chinese coast and the Yangtze River, such as Zhoushan, Ningbo, Wusong and Zhenjiang, were successively attacked by British warships. In August 1842, the Qing Government was forced to sign the Sino-British *Treaty of Nanking*, the first unequal treaty in modern Chinese history. During the following 60 years, the Qing Government opened wide its doors to the outside world. Unequal treaties followed one after another, including the *Treaty of Wanghea* with the United States, the *Treaty of Whampoa* with France, the *Treaty of Aigun* with Russia and the *Treaty of Shimonoseki* with Japan. The treaties contained the humiliating and sovereignty-forfeiting articles on the cession of territory, the payment of indemnities, stationing of foreign garrisons, free missionary activities and open opium trading. The colonialist powers took control of China's Customs administration and rights for tariff agreements. They enjoyed consular jurisdiction and the power to issue bank notes, seizing China's sovereignty by piecemeal encroachment or wholesale annexation. The Chinese people hated the unequal treaties, and when the Boxers rose in rebellion, they declared: "We resent the treaties most because they wreck the country and ruin the people. Officials in subordinate positions follow the example set by their superiors, and the people cannot have their injustice redressed."

英国鸦片商人正监督中国鸦片贩子对他运来的鸦片开箱、过磅。这是当年英国的一份杂志《绘图伦敦新闻》登载的其派驻中国记者画的现场素描。

Chinese opium traders open boxes containing opium and weigh opium under the watch of British merchants. The sketch, published in the British magazine *The Illustrated London News*, was drawn by the magazine's reporter stationed in China.

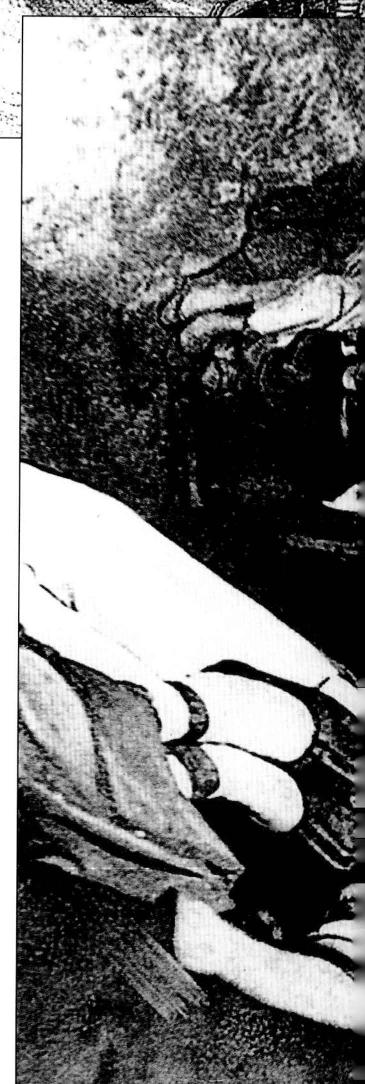

平民烟馆比比皆是，简陋的烟榻上总是横满了吸食鸦片的人。

Opium dens could be seen everywhere. The simple and crude couches were always crowded with opium addicts.

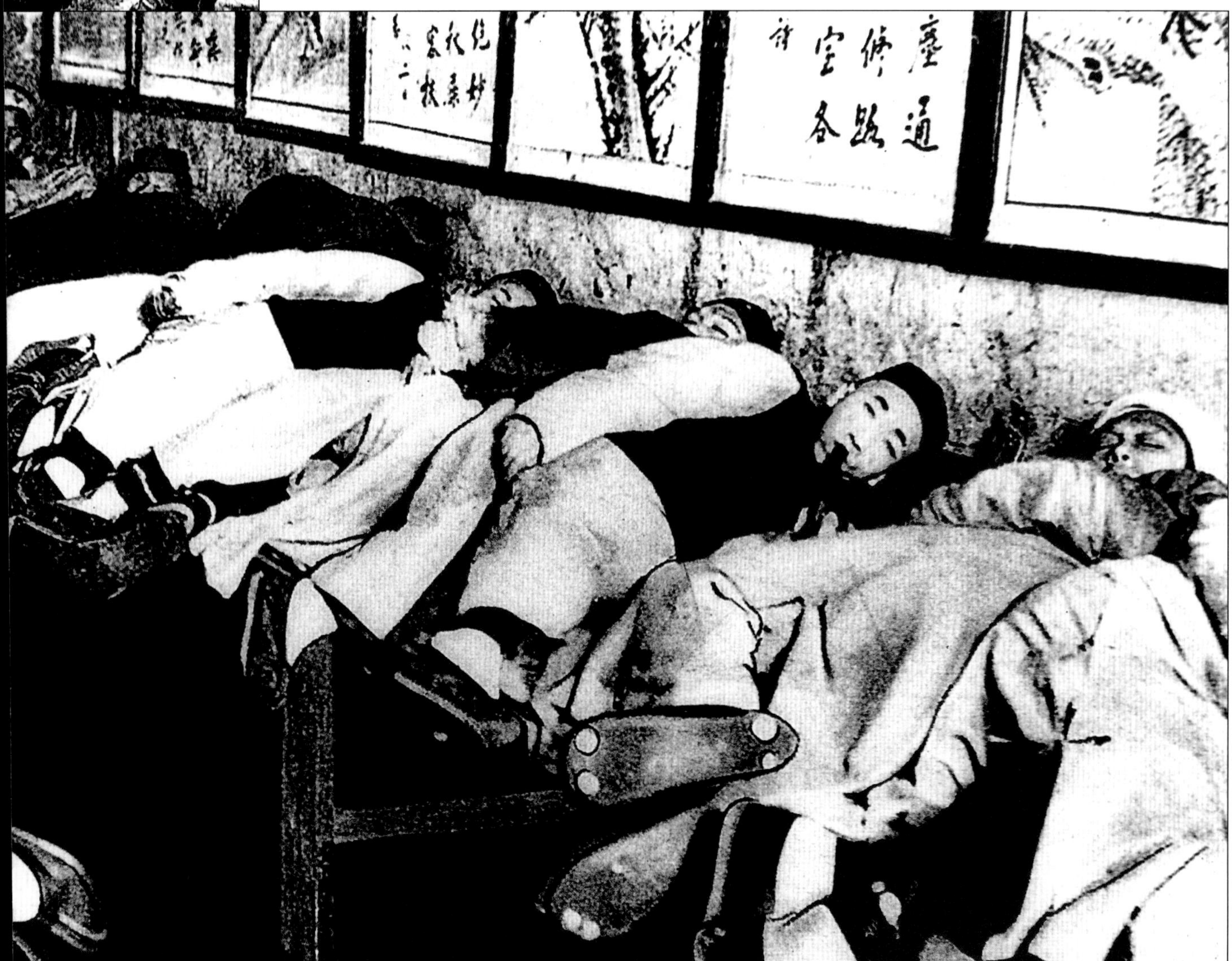

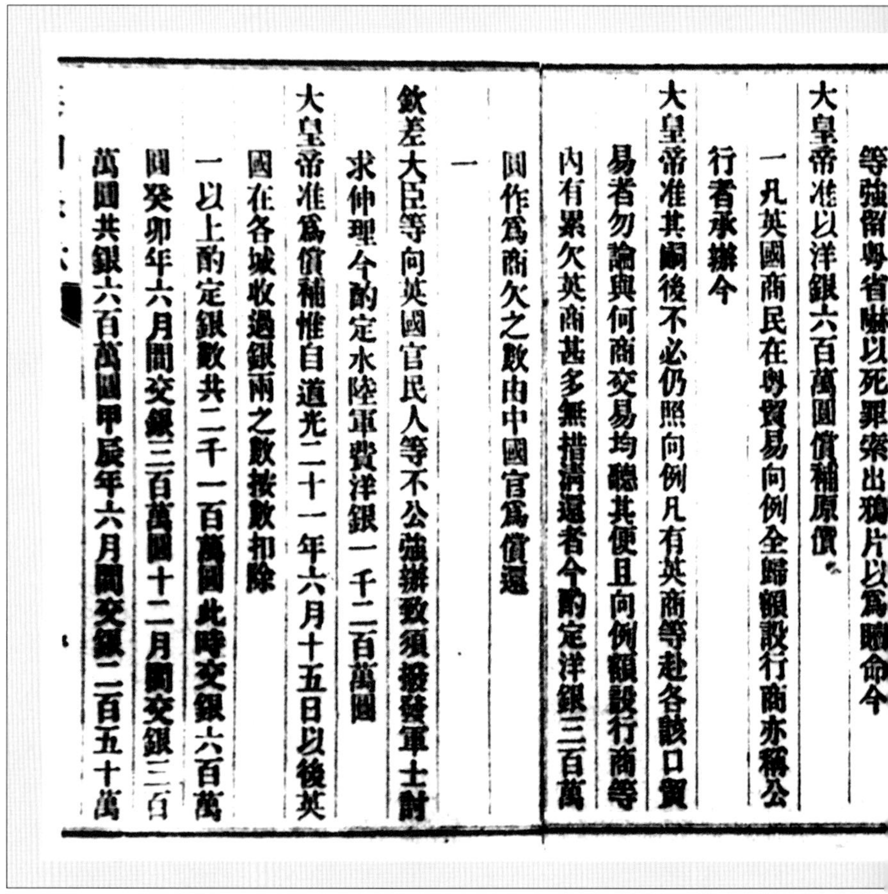

等強留粵省嚇以死罪索出鴉片以為贖命今
大皇帝准以洋銀六百萬圓償補原價。
一　凡英國商民在粵貿易向例全歸額設行商亦稱公
行者承辦今
大皇帝准其嗣後不必仍照向例凡有英商等赴各該口貿
易者勿論與何商交易均聽其便且向例額設行商等
內有累欠英商甚多無措清還者今酌定洋銀三百萬
圓作為商欠之數由中國官為償還
一　欽差大臣等向英國官民人等不公強辦致須撥發軍士討
求伸理今酌定水陸軍費洋銀一千二百萬圓
大皇帝准為償補惟自道光二十一年六月十五日以後英
國在各城收過銀兩之數按數扣除
一　以上酌定銀數共二千一百萬圓此時交銀六百萬
圓癸卯年六月間交銀三百萬圓十二月間交銀三百
萬圓共銀六百萬圓甲辰年六月間交銀二百五十萬

中英《南京条约》文本（局部）。
Text of the *Treaty of Nanking* signed between China and Britain (partial)

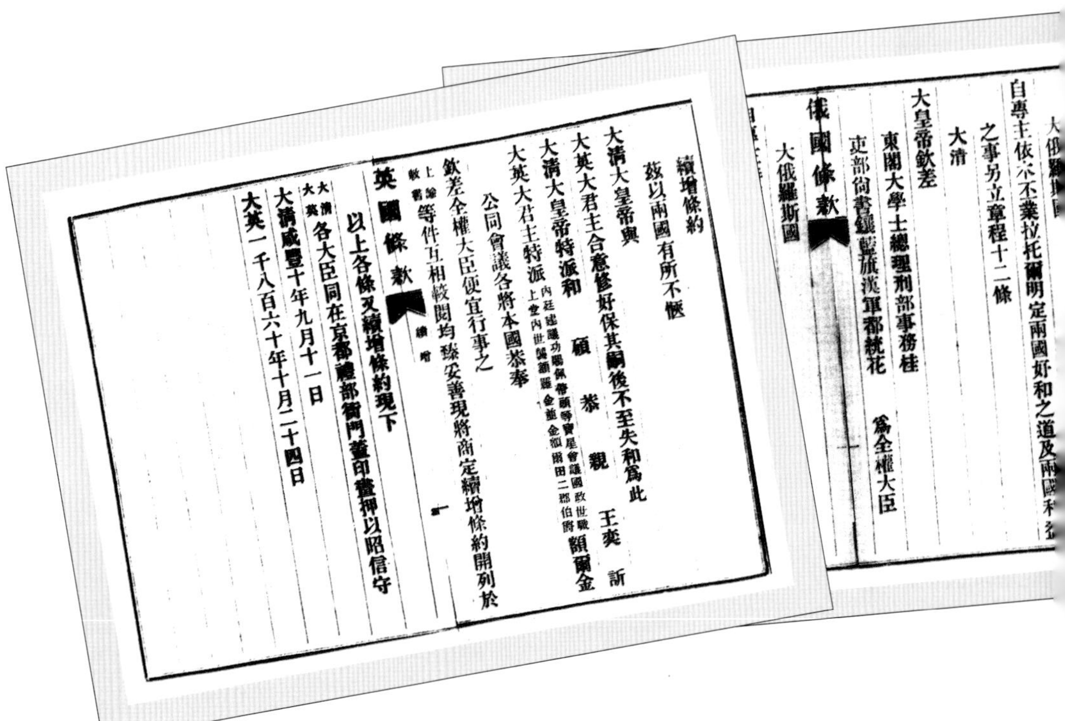

續增條約
茲以兩國有所不愜
大清大皇帝與
大英大君主合意修好保其嗣後不至失和為此
大清大皇帝特派和碩恭親王奕訢
大英大君主特派 額爾金
公同會議各將本國恭奉
欽差全權大臣便宜行事之
上諭 敕書 等件互相較閱均屬妥善現將商定續增條約開列於
英國條款
以上各條又續增條約現下
大清 大英 各大臣同在京都禮部衙門蓋印畫押以昭信守
大清咸豐十年九月十一日
大英一千八百六十年十月二十四日

之事另立章程十二條
大清
大皇帝欽差
東閣大學士總理刑部事務桂
吏部尚書鑲藍旗漢軍都統花　為全權大臣
俄國條款
大俄羅斯國

这是部分不平等条约。
Some of the unequal treaties

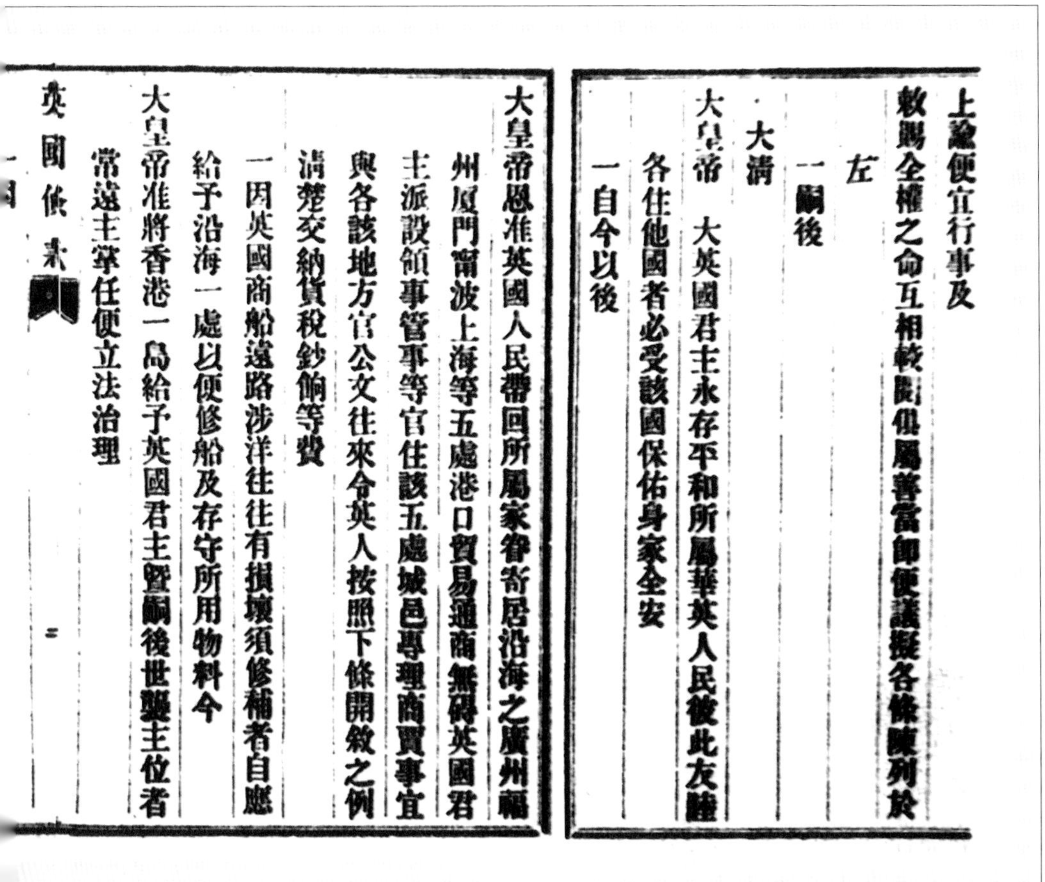

上諭便宜行事及
敕賜全權之命互相較閱俱屬善當即便議擬各條陳列於
左
一嗣後
大清
大皇帝 大英國君主永存平和所屬華英人民彼此友睦
各住他國者必受該國保佑身家全安
一自今以後
大皇帝恩准英國人民帶同所屬家眷寄居沿海之廣州福
州廈門寧波上海等五處港口貿易通商無礙英國君
主派設領事管事等官住該五處城邑專理商賈事宜
與各該地方官公文往來令英人按照下條開敘之例
清楚交納貨稅鈔餉等費
一因英國商船遠路涉洋往往有損壞須修補者自應
給予沿海一處以便修船及存守所用物料今
大皇帝准將香港一島給予英國君主暨嗣後世襲主位者
常遠主掌任便立法治理

英國條款 二

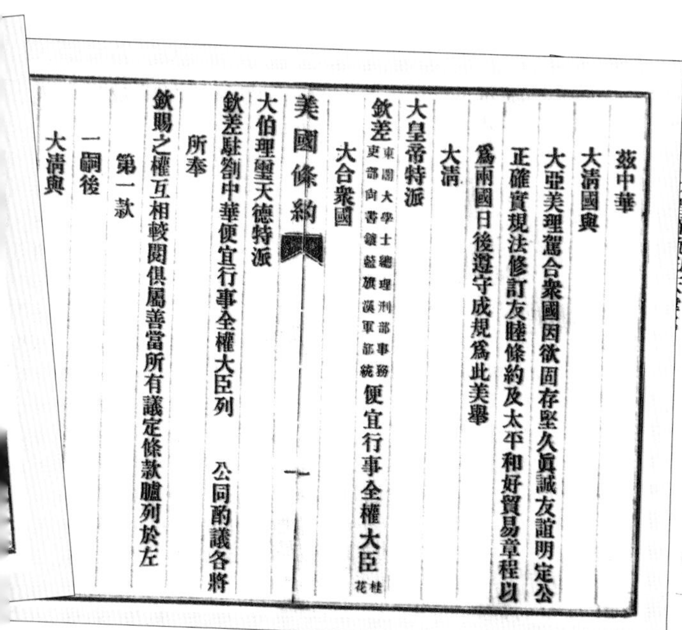

茲中華
大清國與
大亞美理駕合衆國因欲固存堅久真誠友誼明定公
正確實規法修訂友睦條約及太平和好貿易章程以
為兩國日後遵守成規為此美舉
大清
大皇帝特派
欽差東閣大學士總理刑部事務吏部尚書鑲藍旗漢軍都統便宜行事全權大臣桂花
大合衆國
大伯理璽天德特派
欽差駐劄中華便宜行事全權大臣列 公同酌議各將
所奉
欽賜之權互相較閱俱屬善當所有議定條款臚列於左
第一款
一嗣後
大清與

美國條約 一

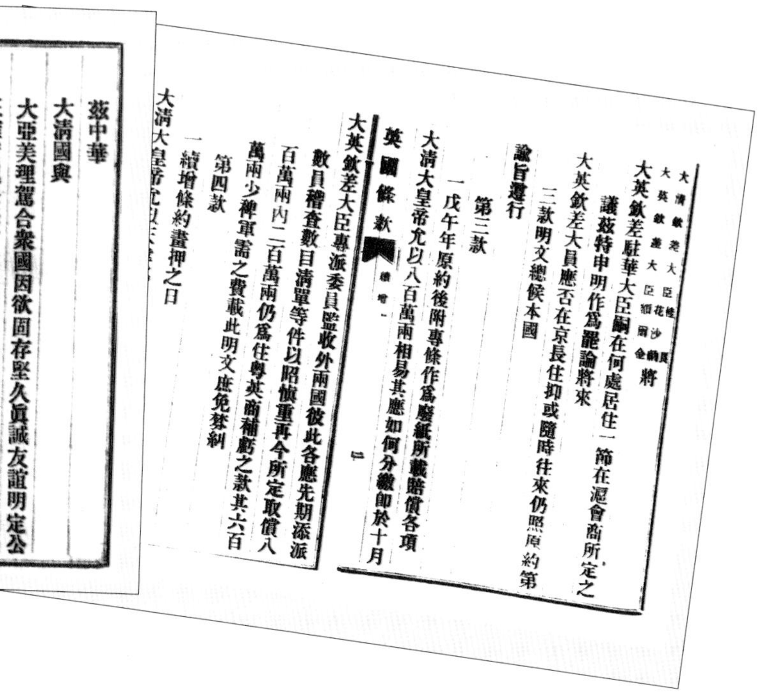

大清欽差大臣桂良花沙納
大英欽差大臣額爾金 將
大英欽差駐華大臣嗣在何處居住一節在滬會商所定之
議茲特申明作為罷論將來
大英欽差大員應否在京長住抑或隨時往來仍照原約第
三款明文總候本國
諭旨遵行
第三款
一戊午年原約後附專條作為廢紙所載賠償各項
大清大皇帝允以八百萬兩相易其應如何分繳即於十月

英國條款 續增 二

大英欽差大臣專派委員監收外兩國彼此各應先期添派
數員稽查數目清單等件以昭慎重再今所定取償八
百萬兩內二百萬兩仍為住粵英商補虧之款其六百
萬兩少裨軍需之費載此明文庶免葛糾
第四款
一續增條約畫押之日
大清大皇帝允以

割　地
Cession of Territory

不平等条约把中国领土分割得面目全非，俄国割去中国150多万平方公里，日本割去台湾、澎湖列岛等地，英国、法国等也抢割了中国的大片土地。

The unequal treaties drastically carved up the Chinese territory. Russia took more than 1.5 million square kilometers of land from China, while Japan took Taiwan and the Penghu Islands. Britain, France and other powers also grabbed large areas of land from China.

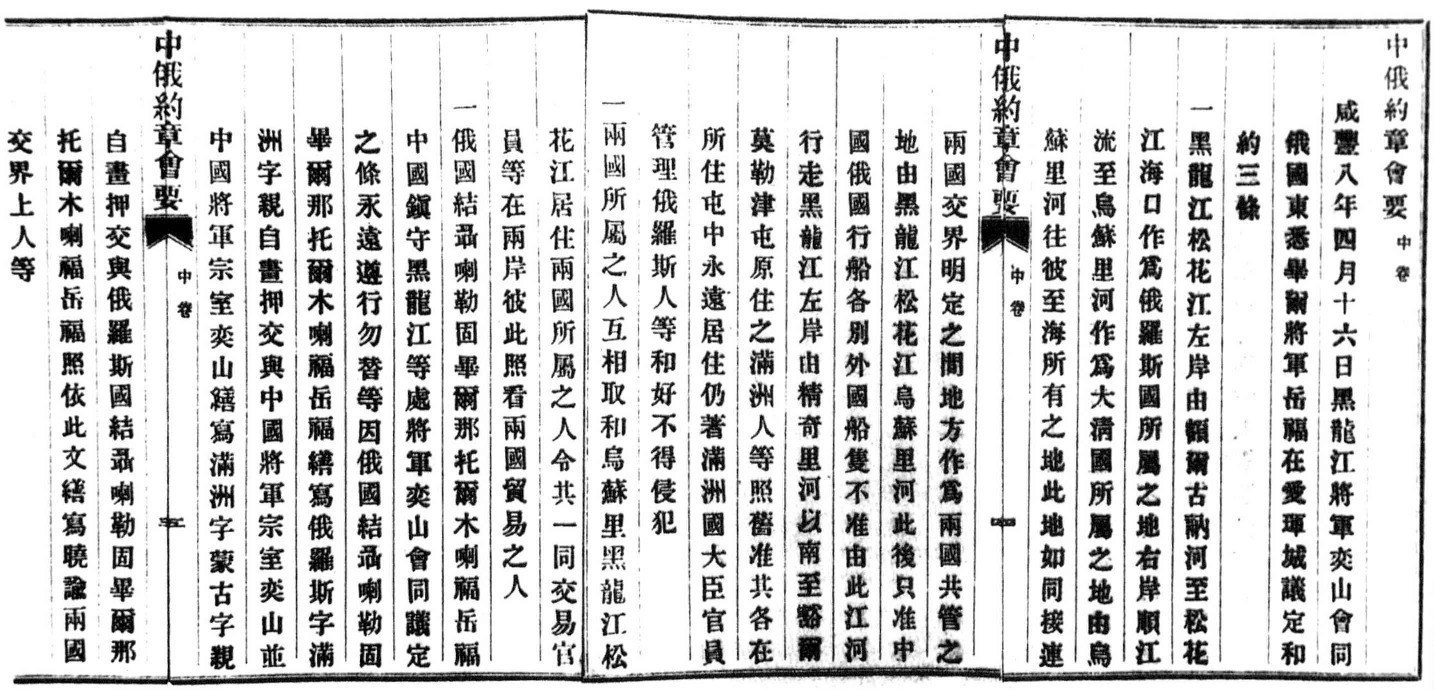

中俄約章會要 中卷

咸豐八年四月十六日黑龍江將軍奕山會同俄國東悉畢爾將軍岳福在愛琿城議定和約三條

一黑龍江松花江左岸由額爾古訥河至松花江海口作爲俄羅斯國所屬之地右岸順江流至烏蘇里河作爲大清國所屬之地由烏蘇里河往彼至海所有之地此地如同接連兩國交界明定之間地方作爲兩國共管之地由黑龍江松花江烏蘇里河此後只准中國俄國行船各別外國船隻不准由此江河行走黑龍江左岸由精奇里河以南至豁爾莫勒津屯原住之滿洲人等照舊准其各在所住屯中永遠居住仍著滿洲國大臣官員管理俄羅斯人等和好不得侵犯

一兩國所屬之人互相取和烏蘇里黑龍江松花江居住兩國所屬之人令其一同交易官員等在兩岸彼此照看兩國貿易之人

一俄國結畾喇勒固畢爾那托爾木喇福岳福中國鎮守黑龍江等處將軍奕山會同議定之條永遠遵行勿替等因俄國結畾喇勒固畢爾那托爾木喇福岳福繕寫俄羅斯字滿洲字親自畫押交與中國將軍宗室奕山並中國將軍宗室奕山繕寫滿洲字蒙古字親自畫押交與俄羅斯國結畾喇勒固畢爾那托爾木喇福岳福照依此文繕寫曉諭兩國交界上人等

中俄約章會要 中卷 一

中俄約章會要 中卷 二

中俄《瑷珲条约》全文。

中俄《瑷珲条约》有关割地的条款。

The articles concerning the cession of territory in the *Treaty of Aigun* signed between China and Russia

▶ 1897年11月1日，在中国山东巨野县，两名传教的德国神甫被当地受教会欺侮的百姓杀死。德国威廉二世电令远东舰队："华人终究给我们提供了期待好久的理由与事件。舰队立即驶往胶州湾，占领该处现有村镇，并采取严厉报复手段。"

次年3月，清政府被迫在中德《胶澳租界条约》签字，德国占有了良港胶州湾和整个山东的开矿权、铁路建设权。

这是威廉二世皇帝与帝国海军官兵合影。

On November 1, 1897, two German priests were killed by locals bullied by the church in Juye County, Shandong Province. German Emperor William II telegraphed the Far East Fleet to the effect that the Chinese finally provided them with the long-waited excuse and event. He ordered that fleet immediately advance toward Jiaozhou Bay to occupy all villages and towns there and take harsh vindictive acts.

In March the following year, the Qing Government was forced to sign the Sino-German treaty on territory concession, by which Germany came into possession of the harbor at Jiaozhou Bay, and procured the rights for mining and railway construction in the whole of Shandong Province.

Here is a photo of William II with German navy officers and men.

俄国炮兵在中国的土地上布炮。

Russians deploying artillery on Chinese soil

领土残破，中国人民失去土地和家园，处于生命无保障，生活无着落的绝望境地。

With fragmentary territories, the Chinese people lost land and homes. They lived in desperation with no security in their lives.

人民流离失所。
Destitute and homeless people

租界与领事裁判权
Concessions and Consular Jurisdiction

1845年11月29日，英国与清政府签下《上海租地章程》，并着手在黄浦江边划出0.56平方公里的土地，开辟租界。自此，列强纷纷在中国各大城市划地，设立租界。到1900年，列强已在广州、汉口、九江、重庆、天津等12城市，设立25处租界。如天津租界占地3平方公里，相当于一个半旧天津城，上海租界占地21平方公里。租界享有独立的行政管理权、司法权，管理租界内的居民（包括中国人）。租界还设立管理机构、税收机构、自建学校、医院、教堂，并设有警局、法院、监狱，甚至驻扎正规军队，还把持了港航权、治河权，地皮拍卖权，并通过征税和庇护走私获取暴利。清政府无权过问租界事务。各国领事是租界的总督，除管理租界内的事务，他们还时时干预租界外中国政府的事务。美国驻上海领事祁理蕴1846年来华办理租界事宜时，曾坦白地说："这种外国领事的专辖权，在欧洲任何国家都不会容许的。"

On November 29, 1845, Britain forced the Qing Government to sign a treaty on land lease in Shanghai, and began carving up 0.56 square kilometers of land by the Huangpu River as a concession. After that, other powers began to grab land in big Chinese cities to set up concessions. By 1900, these powers had set up 25 concessions in 12 cities, including Guangzhou, Hankou, Jiujiang, Chongqing and Tianjin. The concession in Tianjin covered 3 square kilometers, which was equivalent to one and a half of the old Tianjin City, and the concession in Shanghai totaled 21 square kilometers. The concessions enjoyed independent executive and judicial power, and handled affairs relating to all residents in the concessions (including the Chinese). They also had their own administrative and taxation agencies, schools, hospitals, churches, police stations, courts, prisons and even a regular army. The foreign powers controlled inland ports and navigation, river regulations and land auctions. Moreover, they made huge profits through taxation and providing protection to smugglers. The Qing Government was left with no right to look into affairs in the concessions. Foreign consuls were governors of the concessions, who not only managed affairs within the concessions, but also now and then interfered in affairs of the Chinese Government. John N. A. Griswold, US consul in Shanghai, said frankly when he came to China to handle concession-related matters in 1846, "Such jurisdiction enjoyed by foreign consuls is not allowed in any country in Europe."

上海英美租界中的巡捕队。
Police in the British-American concession in Shanghai

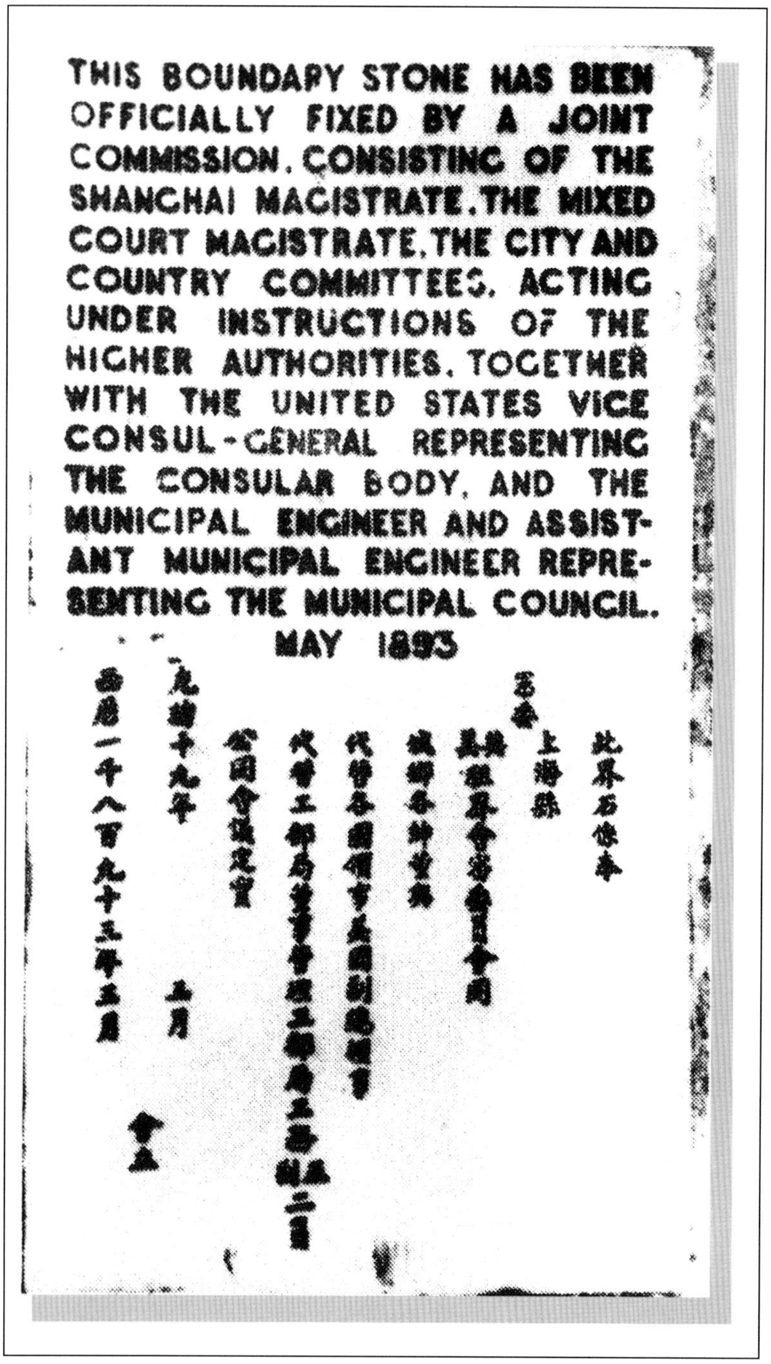

THIS BOUNDARY STONE HAS BEEN OFFICIALLY FIXED BY A JOINT COMMISSION, CONSISTING OF THE SHANGHAI MAGISTRATE, THE MIXED COURT MAGISTRATE, THE CITY AND COUNTRY COMMITTEES, ACTING UNDER INSTRUCTIONS OF THE HIGHER AUTHORITIES, TOGETHER WITH THE UNITED STATES VICE CONSUL-GENERAL REPRESENTING THE CONSULAR BODY, AND THE MUNICIPAL ENGINEER AND ASSISTANT MUNICIPAL ENGINEER REPRESENTING THE MUNICIPAL COUNCIL.

MAY 1893

此界石係奉
上海縣
公同會議定實
光緒十九年 五月
西曆一千八百九十三年五月

上海英美租界1893年竖的界石。此时，这个租界的面积已比当初设立时的830亩扩大了近40倍。

The boundary stone erected in 1893 in the British-American concession in Shanghai. By this time, the concession had expanded nearly 40 times, compared with the initial 0.56 square kilometer area when it was first established.

天津英租界内的维多利亚大街。

Victoria Street in the British concession in Tianjin

被称为戈登府的英租界工部局（租界建设管理部门）办公地。

Gordon Mansion—the office building of the Department of Public Works in the British concession

▲ 天津法租界一角。

A corner of the French concession in Tianjin

▶ 天津法租界通往界外的铁桥。

An iron bridge that linked the French concession with the rest in Tianjin

▲ 天津奥地利租界通往界外的奥地利桥。

The Austrian Bridge connected the Austrian concession with other areas in Tianjin.

1844年7月3日，美国特使顾盛（1800–1879）同样借舰队助威，迫清政府签订了《望厦条约》。在这个条约里，除索到中国关税协定权和美国军舰自由出入中国港口权等，还明确写下了领事裁判权条款。从此，列强压给中国的不平等条约都加上这一条——外国人在中国犯罪或交涉词讼，由其国领事处理，中国官员不得过问。

顾盛向国内报告说：“美国与其他国家，必须感谢英国，因为订立了《南京条约》，开放了中国门户。但现在英国和其他国家也必须感谢美国，因为我们将这门户开放得更宽阔了。”

On July 3, 1844, US Envoy Caleb Cushing (1800-1879), also bolstered by the fleet, forced the Qing Government to sign the *Treaty of Wang-hea*. In addition to the rights for tariff agreement and free entry and exit of American warships at Chinese ports, the treaty explicitly included an article concerning consular jurisdiction. Ever since, all treaties the other powers put on the Chinese added this article–when a foreigner committed a crime or was involved in a lawsuit in China, the case was subject to the jurisdiction of his country's consul in China, and Chinese officials should not interfere. Cushing reported to his country: "The United States and other countries must thank the United Kingdom for signing the *Treaty of Nanking* and opening the door of China. But now the United Kingdom and other countries must also thank the United States for opening the door wider."

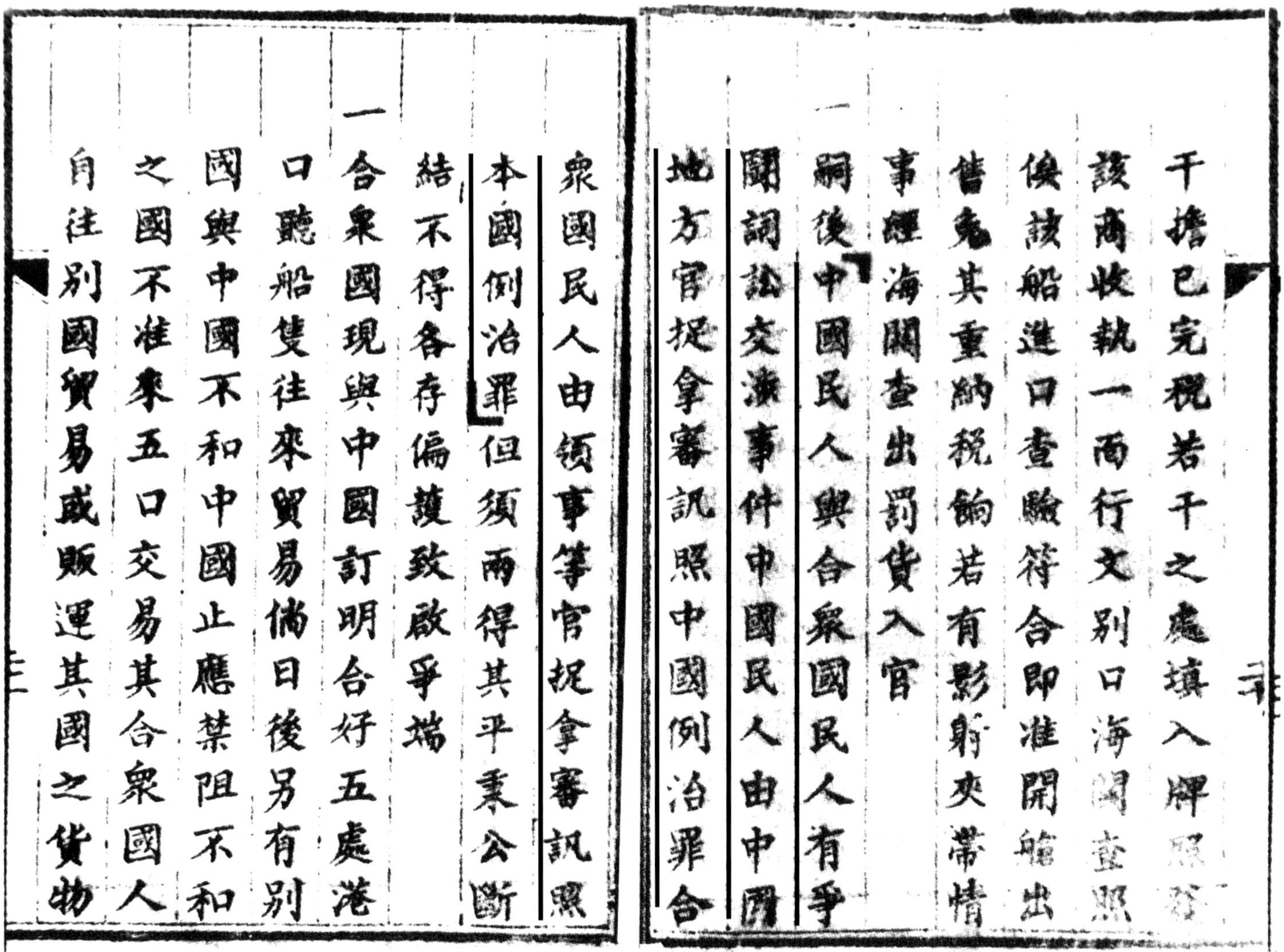
干擔已完稅若干之處填入牌照符
該商收執一面行文別口海關查照
俟該船進口查驗符合即准開艙出
售免其重納稅餉若有影射夾帶情
事經海關查出罰貨入官
一嗣後中國民人與合衆國民人有爭
鬬詞訟交涉事件中國民人由中國
地方官捉拿審訊照中國例治罪合
衆國民人由領事等官捉拿審訊照
本國例治罪但須兩得其平秉公斷
結不得各存偏護致啟爭端
一合衆國現與中國訂明合好五處港
口聽船隻往來貿易倘日後另有別
國與中國不和中國止應禁阻不和
之國不准來五口交易其合衆國人
自往別國貿易或販運其國之貨物

中美《望厦条约》有关领事裁判权的部分内容。（见粗线标出段）

Part of the content of the Sino-US *Treaty of Wang-hea* on consular jurisdiction (See the underlined part)

英国人控制中国海关
Chinese Customs Under British Control

1858年11月，清政府被迫在《天津条约》的补充条款，中英《通商章程善后条约》上签字。条约规定海关要“聘用英国人帮办税务。”5年后，赫德坐上海关头把交椅。此后，英、美、法、德、俄籍人士遍踞总关和分关要职。

海关官员大都眷顾本国，他们参与制订的关税税率，洋货进口按值百抽五的税率纳税，而出口商品——土货却按值百抽八、抽九甚至抽十的比率纳税，出口日弱，进口日强。曾在江浙、两淮和广东做官多年的清政府大员郭嵩焘，描述洋货充斥市场的情形说：“钟表玩具家皆有之，呢绒洋布遍及穷荒僻壤。”如潮涌入的洋货就这样挤垮了中国织造土布、制作烧酒、土蜡等生活用品的千千万万的小作坊、小手工业。中国赴美留学第一人、1850年毕业于耶鲁大学的容闳，在他的著述《西学东渐记》中讲到洋货倾销时，说道：“中国工界乃大受其影响，生计事业，几已十夺其九。”连英国人办的《北华捷报》对中国海关的作法也看不下去了，载文说：“现行制度是荒谬的，……没有一个国家能这样牺牲生产来保护外国的货物。”

In November 1858, the Qing Government was forced to sign a Sino-British agreement containing rules of trade as a supplement to the *Treaties of Tientsin*. It was stipulated that Customs "should employ British to help with taxation." Five years later, Robert Hart occupied the highest post in Customs. After that, the British, Americans, French, Germans and Russians filled important posts in the head and branch offices of Chinese Customs.

Most of the foreign Customs officials cared for their own countries. They participated in the formation of tariff rates: Imported foreign goods were thus taxed at the rate of 5 percent of their value, while local goods for export were taxed at the rate of 8, 9 or even 10 percent. As a result, imports increased rapidly while exports dwindled. Guo Songtao, a high-ranking official of the Qing Government, who held posts in Jiangsu, Zhejiang, areas north and south of the Huaihe River, and Guangdong for many years, described a market glutted with foreign goods in these words: "Every household has clocks, watches and toys, and nylon and imported machine-made cloth can be found even in remote and poor areas." Due to the massive influx of foreign goods, tens of thousands of small local workshops and craft-people making homespun cloth, liquor, wax and other daily necessities went bankrupt. Rong Hong, the first Chinese to study in the United States, who graduated from Yale University in 1850, wrote about the dumping of foreign goods in China in his book entitled *My Life in China and America*. He deplored: "Chinese industry is greatly affected, and about 90 percent of people have lost their means of livelihood."

Even the British-run *North China Herald* could not bear to see this decline in Chinese Customs. One of its articles stated: "The current system is ridiculous...no country can sacrifice production in such a way to protect foreign goods."

赫德（1835–1911）英国人，清政府海关总税务司。1854年来华，在英国驻华外交机构任职。1863年继其同胞李泰国之后，任清政府海关总税务司并被授予太子太保尚书衔，他在这座头把交椅上发号施令了48年。

Englishman Robert Hart (1835-1911) was Inspector-General of Customs of the Qing Government. He came to China in 1854 and held posts in the British diplomatic service in China. In 1863, as successor to his countryman Horatio Nelson Lay, he took office as Inspector-General of Customs of the Qing Government and was conferred the title "Secretary to the Crown Prince." He stayed in the post for 48 years.

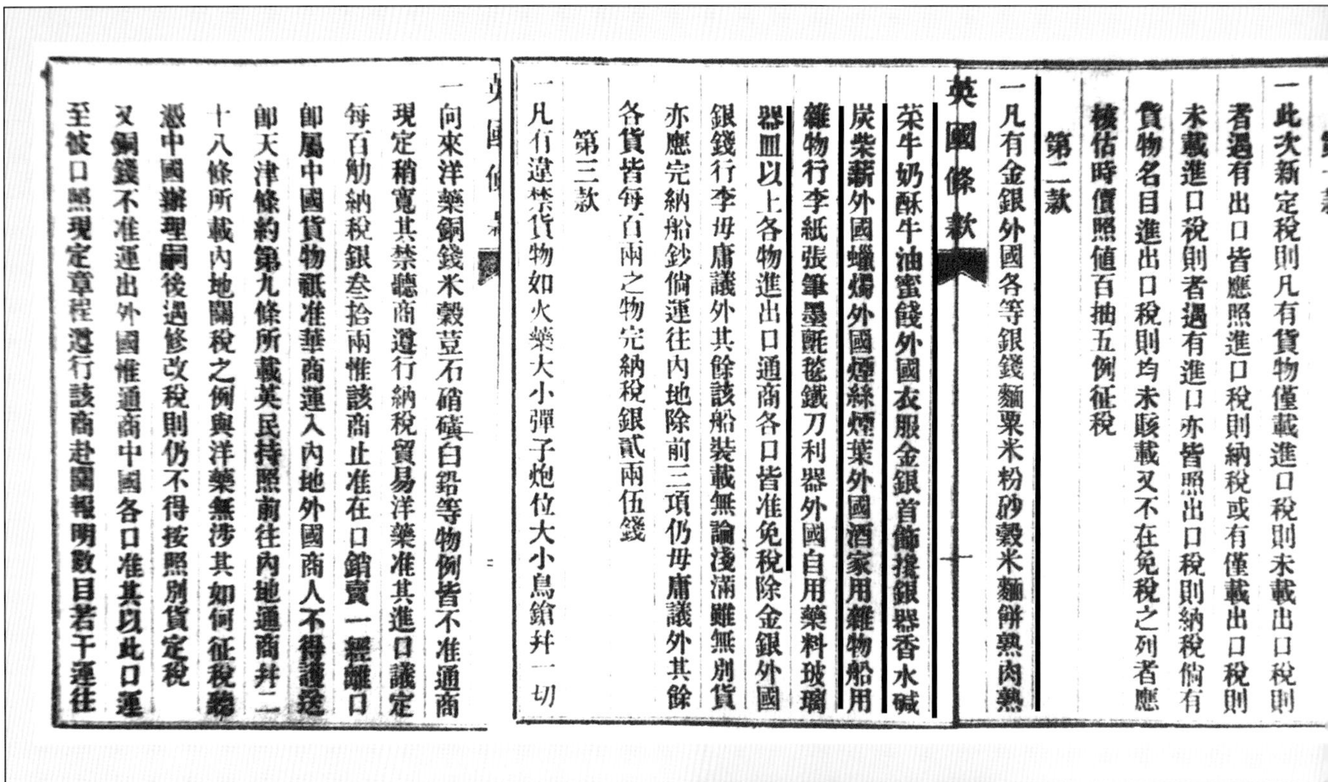

第一款

一此次新定稅則凡有貨物僅載進口稅則未載出口稅則者遇有出口皆應照進口稅則納稅或有僅載出口稅則未載進口稅則者遇有進口亦皆照出口稅則納稅倘有貨物名目進出口稅則均未賅載又不在免稅之列者應核估時價照值百抽五例征稅

第二款

一凡有金銀外國各等銀錢麵粟米粉砂穀米麵餅熟肉熟

英國條款

菜牛奶酥牛油蜜餞外國衣服金銀首飾攙銀器香水碱炭柴薪外國蠟燭外國煙絲煙葉外國酒家用雜物船用雜物行李紙張筆墨氈毯鐵刀利器外國自用藥料玻璃器皿以上各物進出口通商各口皆准免稅除金銀外國銀錢行李毋庸議外其餘該船裝載無論淺滿雖無別貨亦應完納船鈔倘運往內地除前三項仍毋庸議外其餘各貨皆每百兩之物完納稅銀貳兩伍錢

第三款

一凡有違禁貨物如火藥大小彈子炮位大小鳥鎗并一切

英國條款

一向來洋藥銅錢米穀荳石硝磺白鉛等物例皆不准通商現定稍寬其禁聽商遵行納稅貿易洋藥准其進口議定每百觔納稅銀叁拾兩惟該商止准在口銷賣一經離口即屬中國貨物衹准華商運入內地外國商人不得護送即天津條約第九條所載英民持照前往內地通商并二十八條所載內地關稅之例與洋藥無涉其如何征稅聽憑中國辦理嗣後遇修改稅則仍不得按照別貨定稅又銅錢不准運出外國惟通商中國各口准其以此口運至彼口照現定章程遵行該商赴關報明數目若干運往

金、银、货币、烟、酒、洋药……类似商品，被各国海关视为禁品或课以重税。但在 1858 年的中英《天津条约》里，明文规定上述商品与其他的几十种商品一样免税，进入中国海关。(见条约中粗线标出段)

Goods like gold, silver, currency, tobacco, liquor and foreign drugs were regarded by the Customs of other countries as banned goods, or items for heavy taxation. But in the Sino-British *Treaty of Tientsin* signed in 1858, it was explicitly stipulated that the aforementioned goods were exempt from import duties when they entered into China, like dozens of other commodities. (See the underlined part)

洋货从天津海关登陆，运销华北城乡。这是繁忙的天津码头。

Foreign goods entered China through Tianjin Customs before being transported to urban and rural areas in north China. Here is a scene of the bustling Tianjin dock.

失业者临时下冰窖打工。

The unemployed worked part time in an icehouse.

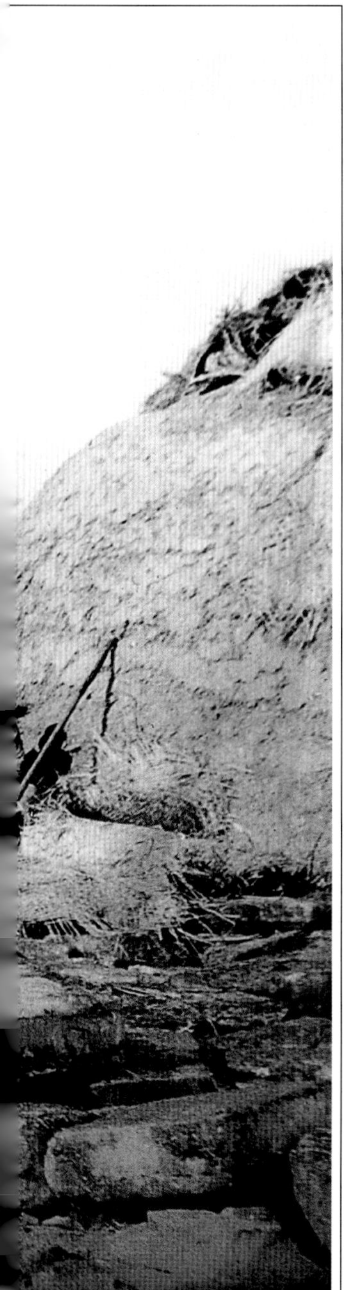

这条破船也撑不过几时了。
This wretched boat could hardly hold up any longer.

银　行
Banks

1845年，世界首强英国，未经清政府准许，在上海租界开设了第一家银行——丽如银行，吸收中国人存储，转贷给在华的英国商行，扩大对华贸易。到十九世纪末，法、德、日、俄、比等国均在华设立了银行。这些同样未获清政府允办的银行，甚至行使一国中央银行的职能：垄断汇兑、发行纸币……主宰了中国的金融市场。为追逐高额利润，这些银行在铁路和矿山投资中展开竞争，并争相包办清政府的巨额借款。1894年中日战争，清政府告败，为支付给日本赔款2.315亿两白银，清政府被迫向外举债。俄国、法国联手争得了1亿两白银的头笔借款权。这笔贷款年息4厘，34年还清，算上折扣，届时，两国利息收入即高达1.17亿两白银。英国汇丰银行和德国德华银行联手与清政府交涉，于1896年争到了1亿两白银的借款权。1897年争到了另1亿两白银的借款权，年息4.5厘，按八三折扣付银——名义借出1亿两白银，实际只支付8300万两，规定45年还清，总利息比本金还多。为追求高利息，借款合同限定清政府“不得加速偿还或提前一次还清借款”。

此时，清政府主管财政的户部衙门，尚无一家银行，中国的财政命脉被外国银行掌握。

In 1845, Britain, the most powerful nation in the world at that time, opened the Oriental Bank, the first bank in Shanghai's concession, without authorization of the Qing Government. The bank absorbed savings deposits from the Chinese and extended loans to British firms in China to expand British trade. By the end of the 19th century, France, Germany, Japan, Russia, Belgium and other nations had all set up banks in China. None of these banks had authorization from the Qing Government, yet they exercised functions of the central bank, including monopolizing exchange and issuing bank notes, thus controlling China's financial market. To secure high profits, these banks competed with one another in railway and mining investments, and vied with each other in contracting huge loans of the Qing Government. To pay Japan indemnities of 231.5 million taels of silver after its defeat during the 1894 Sino-Japanese War, the Qing Government had to secure foreign loans. Russia and France joined together to procure the right for the first loan of 100 million taels of silver. This loan, with an annual interest rate of 4 percent, was scheduled to be repaid in 34 years. While taking discounts into account, the two countries would gain 117 million taels of silver in interest by the time the loan was repaid. The British Hong Kong-Shanghai Banking Corporation (HSBC) allied with the German Deutsch Asiatische Bank in negotiations with the Qing Government and in 1896, they obtained the right to extend loans amounting to 100 million taels of silver. In 1897, they obtained the right to extend another loan of 100 million taels of silver, the annual interest rate being 4.5 percent. The loan was extended with 17 percent discount–nominally the loan was 100 million taels of silver, but actually the Qing Government only received 83 million taels of silver. It was agreed that the loan would be repaid in 45 years. The aggregate interest exceeded the amount of the principal. To secure high profits, the loan contract particularly stipulated that the Qing Government "shall not quicken its pace of repayment or make a lump-sum repayment in advance."

At the time, however, the Ministry of Revenue of the Qing Government in charge of finance didn't open a single bank. China's financial lifeblood was completely in the hands of foreign banks.

汇丰银行1865年在上海开业，远在英国的伦敦委员会是其最高决策机构。依仗不平等条约，汇丰在华发展十分迅速。1877年，陕甘总督左宗棠用兵西北，向汇丰借贷1075万两白银，年息高达15厘（15%）。通过类似贷款和发行钞票及控制汇价，"汇丰"赚到丰厚利润，并取得了中国关税及部分省市盐税、常税的收存权。赫德担任中国海关最高首脑近半个世纪，英国获取沪宁、广九、沪杭甬、津浦南段铁路的筑路权都与"汇丰"的支持密切相关。1865年，汇丰在华吸收存款折合港币仅300万元，到八国联军进攻北京这一年，存款总额折合港币已逾亿元。被称为执中国金融市场牛耳的龙头银行。

The HSBC started operation in Shanghai in 1865, with the London Committee in Britain being its supreme decision-maker. Backed by the unequal treaties, the HSBC developed rapidly in China. In 1877, when Zuo Zongtang, Governor-General of Shaanxi and Gansu, had military actions in northwest China, he borrowed 10.75 million taels of silver from the HSBC, with an annual interest rate as high as 15 percent. Through such types of loans, the issue of bank notes and control of the exchange rate, the HSBC earned huge profits and obtained the power to receive and keep tariffs of the Chinese Government, as well as salt tax and regular taxes in some provinces and cities. The occupation of the highest post in Chinese Customs by Robert Hart for nearly half a century, and the procurement of the rights for constructing the Shanghai-Nanjing, Guangzhou-Kowloon, Shanghai-Hangzhou-Ningbo and Tianjin-Pukou (southern section) railways were all closely related to the support of the HSBC. In 1865, savings deposits absorbed by the HSBC in China were only 3 million HK dollars, which exceeded 100 million HK dollars by the time the Eight-Power Allied Forces attacked Beijing. The HSBC was regarded as the leading bank in China's financial market.

德国德华银行，1889年入华设行，发行的货币流通于山东省，是胶济铁路的主要投资者。这是其在北京的办公大楼。

The Deutsch Asiatische Bank of Germany set up an office in China in 1889 and currency issued by the bank circulated in Shandong Province. It was a major investor of the Qingdao-Jinan Railway. Pictured here is the office building of the bank in Beijing.

1893年进入中国的日本横滨正金银行在北京的列强银行中也占一席之地。

The Japanese Yokohama Specie Bank, which entered China in 1893, also held a portion of the banking business in Beijing.

建筑铁路带来的权益和利润极大。列强的在华银行，鼎力支持本国争夺铁路筑路权。到十九世纪末，英国获得的筑路权2800英里、俄国1530英里、德国720英里、法国420英里、美国300英里。

Railway construction brought about enormous profits. All foreign banks in China used their influence to help their own countries seize the right to construct railways. By the end of the 19th century, Britain had obtained rights for the construction of 2,800 miles of railways; Russia, 1,530 miles; Germany, 720 miles; France, 420 miles; and the United States, 300 miles.

铁路修到了北京城下。

Railways were built to the city wall of Beijing.

铁路运费大大低于河运，京杭运河渐趋清冷。

As rail transportation cost much less than water transportation, business on the Beijing-Hangzhou Canal gradually declined.

赔款
Indemnities

列强借不平等条约向清政府索取巨额赔款，从1840年到1895年，仅《南京条约》、《北京条约》、《马关条约》就赔付白银26850万两。

Taking advantage of the unequal treaties, foreign powers demanded huge amounts of indemnities from the Qing Government. From 1840 to 1895, the Qing Government paid indemnities totaling 268.5 million taels of silver according to the *Treaty of Nanking*, the *Convention of Peking* and the *Treaty of Shimonoseki*.

1894年6月，日本入侵朝鲜，迅即把战火燃进中国，占领了整个辽东半岛，并经黄海、威海两次海战，消灭了清政府北洋舰队。次年4月17日，就在这里——日本山口县下关（也称马关）市的春帆楼，清政府代表被迫承认，以割地、赔款等为主要内容的媾和条约，史称《马关条约》。

In June 1894, Japan invaded Korea. Shortly afterward the flames of war spread to China, and Japan occupied the Liaodong Peninsula in the northeast of the country. Through two naval battles on the Yellow Sea and at Weihai, Japan destroyed the Northern Fleet of the Qing Government. On April 17 the following year, representatives of the Qing Government were forced to sign a peace treaty concerning territory cession and indemnities in Japan's Shimonoseki, as shown in the picture. The treaty was historically known as the *Treaty of Shimonoseki*.

这是《绘图伦敦新闻》当年登载的一幅写实画。这幅记者自中国发回的钢笔画，描绘了清政府支付赔银的场景。

This sketch, published in *The Illustrated London News*, and sent by a reporter from China, depicted the payment of indemnities by the Qing Government.

教 会

Churches

八国联军侵华前，据清政府的统计，天主教、基督教、东正教在华的外籍传教士已有3200多人，入教的中国人达80余万，教堂遍布全国城乡。教士享有外交豁免权和种种特权，不少教士无视中国法律，威逼中国官吏，霸占田产，擅自征税，甚至动辄伤人害命。法国神甫马赖、文乃尔、意大利神甫郭西德等人都在传教地作恶累累。梵蒂冈教廷2000年却册封他们为圣人。当年，联军统帅瓦德西都说："关于英美教会事业，余实不能详细批评，但余却深信……所委任之牧师，往往其人德性方面既不相称，职务方面亦未经训练……余更熟知许多牧师，兼作他项营业，如买卖土地，投机事业，实与所任职务全不相称"（见《瓦德西回忆录》）。一些品质恶劣的教民依仗教会势力，鱼肉乡里。当时中国，几乎有教会的地方就有教士、教民与不信教百姓冲突致伤的案件，"教案"一词始出现在汉语文牍中。

Statistics of the Qing Government showed that there were more than 3,200 foreign missionaries of the Catholic, Protestant and Orthodox Eastern Church in China prior to the invasion of the Eight-Power Allied Forces. More than 800,000 Chinese adopted Christianity and churches were scattered throughout cities and the countryside. As foreign missionaries enjoyed diplomatic immunity and various other privileges, many of them defied Chinese laws, threatened Chinese officials, forcibly occupied land and property, arbitrarily levied taxes, and even injured and killed people on the slightest pretext. French priests Auguste Chapdelaine, Jean-Pierre Neel and Italian priest Albericus Crescitelli indulged in all sorts of evildoings in their respective parishes in China. These people, however, were conferred the title of Saint by the Vatican in 2000. Even Alfred Graf von Waldersee, commander-in-chief of the Allied Forces, noted: "With regard to the British and American missionary undertakings, I can't give my criticism in detail. But I firmly believe...appointed missionaries usually lack personal integrity as well as due training in match with their posts....I know well that many missionaries are engaged in other undertakings, such as the buying and selling of land and other speculative activities, which bear no relation to their posts" (*Memoirs of Waldersee*). Some Chinese converts relied on the power of the church to victimize people. In those days, wherever there were churches, there were conflicts between Chinese who did not believe in Christianity, and missionaries and converts. The term "religious case" began to occur in Chinese documents. This, according to historians, constituted an important reason for the Boxer Uprising, whose mission was "to drive foreigners out of Chinese territory and extinguish the churches."

这是法国天主教北京西什库教堂，距紫禁城西北不足两公里，时人称为北堂。它和它的主人樊国梁神甫，在八国联军侵华前后都有可记述的事。

The Pehtang Cathedral in Beijing, founded by the French, was less than two kilometers from the Forbidden City. Both the church and its priest Father Favier were the subjects of many stories before and after the invasion by the Eight-Power Allied Forces.

北京八面槽教堂。
Bamiancao Church in Beijing

建在山东农村的小教堂。
A small church in the country-side in Shandong Province

洋教士在中国乡间传教。
Western missionaries doing missionary work in the countryside of China

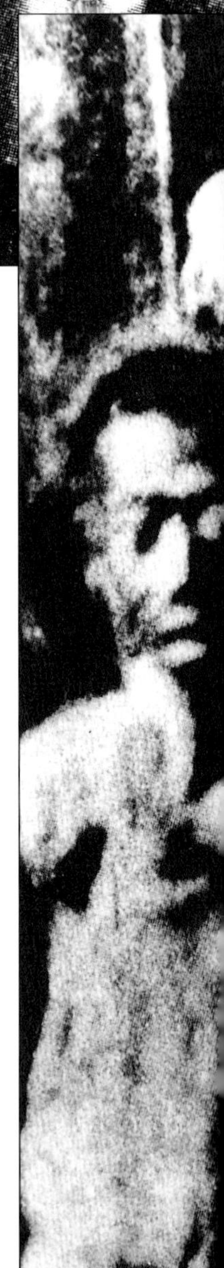

▶ 19世纪末，山东省已有大小教堂1300多座，教会势力很大，不断发生教会强占庙产，伤人害命刑事案件，地方政府不敢干预，于是负冤的庄稼汉们拿起锄头、大刀，号称义和团，向作恶行凶的教士、教民进行报复。义和团张贴告示，指责教会"祸乱中华，耗费国帑，拆庙宇，毁佛像、占民坟，万恶痛恨。"解释自己的旗号说："义者仁也，和者礼也。"表示按老祖宗的道德标准行事。义和团也和以往中国历朝、历代的农民暴动一样，借助了请神附体、念咒画符，号称刀枪不入等迷信方式，很快就把富有敬天、爱国、重视祖宗精神的成千上万的种田人和各阶层人物聚集起来，从山东而至华北、东北，迅速发展成百十万人的运动，一些乡村、城镇相继发生了烧教堂、驱教士、杀教民的冲突。

At the end of the 19th century, there were more than 1,300 churches of different sizes in Shandong Province, which were very powerful. There were constant occurrences of criminal cases in which the churches forcibly took property and injured or killed people. As the local government dared not interfere in these matters, angry peasants took hoes and broad swords in their own hands and, calling themselves the Boxers, took revenge on evildoing missionaries and converts. The Boxers posted notices, accusing the churches of "causing disastrous disorder in China, wasting national wealth, demolishing temples, destroying Buddhist statues and occupying civilian graveyards, which had evoked resentment and hatred among all the people." They explained their slogan

传教士和中国教民。
A missionary and Chinese converts

saying, "justice is benevolence and harmony is propriety," which meant they acted in accordance with moral standards set by the ancestors. Like previous peasant rebellions in Chinese history, the Boxers also employed superstitious means, such as inviting spirits to enter the human body, drawing magic characters and reciting incantations, and claiming themselves to be invulnerable to death or injury by spears, sword or bullets. Soon tens of thousands of peasants and people from all walks of life, who were patriotic and respectful of Heaven and ancestors, got together. The Boxer Uprising quickly spread to north and northeast China and involved approximately 1 million people. In some villages and towns, conflicts that occurred were often characterized by the burning down of churches, the dislodging of missionaries and the killing of Chinese Christians.

The En

公使与使馆卫队进京

ing of Envoys and Legation Guards Into Beijing

1899年义和团在山东一出现，清政府即派兵镇压。当义和团打出“扶清灭洋”旗号后，清政府的态度转剿为抚。随着列强对义和团的态度越来越强硬，清政府的态度也在剿抚之间摇摆不定。1900年，当列强一批武装卫队开入北京使馆区，列强八国组成联军，清政府才停止进攻义和团，笼络他们一致对外。

随后，北京发生了多起使馆卫队袭击义和团的流血事件，此时，联军又攻陷天津东南的大沽炮台，义和团在一部分清军的参与下，开始围攻使馆和教堂。

When the Boxer Uprising first broke out in Shandong Province in 1899, the Qing Government immediately sent troops to put down the rebellion. But when the Boxers upheld the slogan of "supporting the Qing and exterminating the foreigners," the Qing Government reversed its attitude from suppression to pacification. However, as the foreign powers took an increasingly intransigent attitude toward the Boxers, the Qing Government vacillated between suppression and pacification. In 1900, when a group of armed legation guards entered the legation quarters in Beijing and the eight powers formed allied forces, the Qing Government stopped attacking the Boxers and united with them against the foreigners.

After that, a number of sanguinary events occurred in Beijing, in which the legation guards attacked the Boxers. Meanwhile, Allied Forces captured Dagu Fort in southeast Tianjin. The Boxers, together with Qing troops, began to lay siege to legations and churches.

被清政府任命为山东巡抚的袁世凯，上任即逐村搜捕义和团民，斩首数千，时人称之为“袁屠夫”。

After he took office, Yuan Shikai, Governor of Shandong Province, searched village after village for the Boxers and beheaded thousands of them. Hence Yuan's nickname "Butcher Yuan."

义和团团民被斩首示众，这种惨景1900年5月前，在山东、直隶两省处处可见。

The Boxers' heads were cut off and shown to the public as a warning to all--a common scene in Shandong and Zhili provinces prior to May 1900.

▼ 直隶省长新镇“坎”字部义和团，模仿官府的虎头牌，树起书有“旨”字的团牌，合法地扩大队伍。

The Boxer division under the character "kan" in Changxin Town, Zhili Province, imitated the tiger-head mark of the government and held the signboard inscribed with "zhi" (meaning imperial edict) to legitimately expand its ranks.

不久，清政府内部以亲王载漪为首的一批守旧官员转而支持义和团。这些官员历来仇视一切洋人、洋事物，现在要借义和团惩罚洋人。他们说服当政的慈禧太后，暂停对团民剿杀，并打出“奉旨办团”的旗号，笼络义和团。千方百计打击光绪皇帝，想让自己儿子取而代之的这位亲王，也在自己的王府设立了拳坛。

Soon after, a group of conservative officials within the Qing Government, headed by Prince Zai Yi, turned to support the Boxers. These officials, who had been hostile to all foreigners and anything foreign, schemed to punish the foreigners by using the force of the Boxers. They convinced Empress Dowager Cixi to suspend the suppression of the Boxers. Under the pretext of "organizing Boxers according to the imperial edict," they drew them over. Zai Yi, who tried every possible means to weaken Emperor Guangxu in the hope that his own son could succeed the throne, also set up a Boxer Altar in his own palace.

进入1900年，各国驻京公使见义和团逼近京城，遂于1月23日、3月10日和4月6日三次发照会或声明，令清政府限期消灭义和团，否则，他们将“领兵代为平叛。”
In 1900, seeing the Boxers were approaching the capital, foreign envoys in Beijing delivered notes or announced statements three times on January 23, March 10 and April 6, respectively. They demanded the Qing Government annihilate the Boxers within a given time; otherwise, they would "lead the army to do the suppression on behalf of the Qing Government."

清政府闭关200年，不知外交惯例，不肯向洋人开放天津，更不允许外国遣公使驻京。1858年、1860年，英法联军两次对华发动战争，最终打进北京，将圆明园毁之一炬。
The Qing Government, which had closed the borders for 200 years, had no knowledge of diplomatic practices. It was unwilling to open Tianjin to foreigners, let alone allow foreign envoys to stay in the capital. In 1858 and 1860, the British-French Allied Forces waged two major wars against China, forcing their way into Beijing and setting fire on Yuan Ming Yuan (the old Summer Palace).

1860年，清政府与英法签署《天津条约》，允许在北京设立使馆。（见条约中粗线标出段）

In 1860, the Qing Government signed the *Treaties of Tientsin* with Britain and France, allowing them to set up legations in Beijing. (See the underlined part)

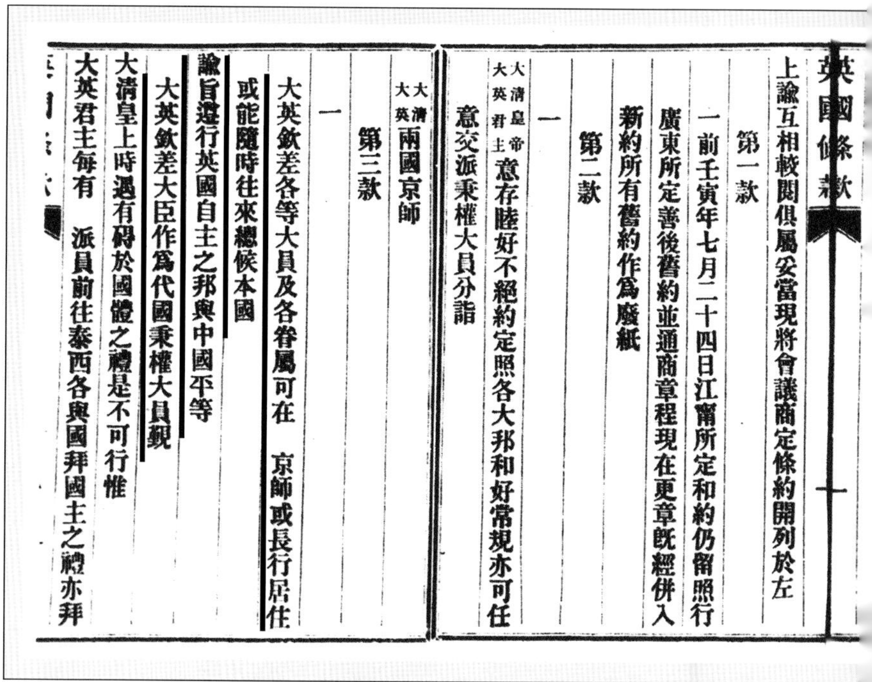

英國條款

上諭互相較閱俱屬妥當現將會議商定條約開列於左

第一款

一前壬寅年七月二十四日江甯所定和約仍留照行

廣東所定善後舊約並通商章程現在更章既經併入

新約所有舊約作為廢紙

第二款

一

大清皇帝 大英君主 意存睦好不絕約定照各大邦和好常規亦可任

意交派秉權大員分詣

大清 大英 兩國京師

第三款

一

大英欽差各等大員及各眷屬可在 京師或長行居住

或能隨時往來總候本國

諭旨遵行英國自主之邦與中國平等

大英欽差大臣作為代國秉權大員覲

大清皇上時遇有碍於國體之禮是不可行惟

大英君主每有 派員前往泰西各與國拜國主之禮亦拜

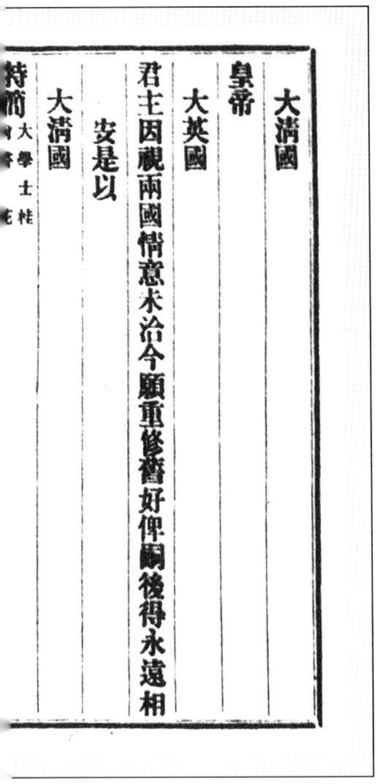

大清國
皇帝
大英國
君主因視兩國情意未洽今願重修舊好俾嗣後得永遠相
安是以
大清國
特簡 大學士桂

英国公使馆
British Legation.

1861年，英法两国公使进入北京，在距紫禁城仅千余米的东交民巷率先设立使馆。之后，俄、日、美、德、奥、西、意、荷、比等国也陆续在这里开馆。

In 1861, British and French envoys entered Beijing and took the lead in setting up legations in Dongjiaominxiang, just 1,000 meters from the Forbidden City. Afterwards, Russia, Japan, the United States, Germany, Austria, Spain, Italy, Holland and Belgium also set up legations here.

▲奥地利公使馆
Austrian Legation

▶日本公使馆
Japanese Legation

◀美国公使馆
The US Legation

▼俄国公使馆
Russian Legation

▶ 德国公使馆
German Legation

▲ 法国公使馆
French Legation

▼意大利公使馆
Italian Legation

樊国梁(1837-1905)法国人，北京西什库教堂（北堂）主教。1899年被派为法国天主教驻北京总主教。清政府特赐他二品官员的服饰，以示礼遇。1900年5月18日，得知距京100多公里的保定府教会与义和团发生流血冲突，他就请求法国政府派兵保护。法国公使即与英、美、俄、德、日、意、奥、西、葡、比等国驻京公使协商，决定自天津调兵到北京，组建使馆卫队。辛丑条约签订后，樊国梁神甫获罗马教廷“宗教卫士”称誉，法国政府也授予他“十字荣誉勋章”。

Frenchman Pierre Marie Alphonse Favier (1873-1905) was bishop of Beijing's Pehtang Cathedral. In 1899, he was appointed chief bishop of French Catholicism in Beijing. The Qing Government granted him the official uniform of the second rank as an indication of courteous reception. On May 18, 1900, being informed of the sanguinary conflict between the Boxers and the church in Baoding Prefecture, about 100 kilometers from Beijing, he requested the French Government send troops for protection. The French envoy discussed this with the envoys of Britain, the United States, Russia, Germany, Japan, Italy, Austria, Spain, Portugal and Belgium in Beijing, and decided to move troops from Tianjin to Beijing to organize legation guards. After the signing of the *Protocol of 1901*, the Roman Catholic Church conferred the title "Religious Guard" to Favier, while the French Government granted him a medal.

1900年5月28日，公使团照会负责外交事务的清政府总理各国事务衙门说，已决定自天津调兵进京，保护使馆和侨民，要求清政府必须同意并提供运输便利。31日晨，清政府同意了公使团的要求。

图为总理各国事务衙门。

On May 28, 1900, the envoys notified the Office for the Management of Business of All Foreign Countries, which was in charge of foreign affairs of the Qing Government, that they had decided to move troops from Tianjin to Beijing to protect the legations and foreign nationals. They demanded the Qing Government give consent and provide transport. On the morning of May 31, the Qing Government gave its consent to the envoys' requirements.

Pictured here is the seat of the Office for the Management of Business of All Foreign Countries.

1900年5月31日，就在清政府发出照会同意洋兵进京的当天，由英、美、法、日、俄、意等国300余名军人组成的第一批使馆卫队，携炮自天津乘火车进入北京。一周后，使馆区的兵力已达1000余人。图为装备精良的英国使馆卫队。

On May 31, 1900, the day when the Qing Government issued the note approving entry of foreign troops into Beijing, the first group of more than 300 legation guards, representing such countries as Britain, the United States, France, Japan, Russia and Italy, traveled by train from Tianjin to Beijing with their cannons. A week later, the force in the legation quarters exceeded 1,000. Pictured here are the well-equipped guards of the British legation.

日本的公使馆卫队。
Guards of the Japanese legation

美国使馆的卫队哨兵在了望。
A guard of the US legation keeps a lookout.

远赴中国参战的德国军队登舰前，威廉二世皇帝训话。

William II making a speech before German troops boarded warships heading for China

日本海军陆战队抢先开进中国，他们后来成了联军主力。

The Japanese Marine Corps were the first to arrive in China. They later became the main strength of the Allied Forces.

亲历1900年事件的英国记者辛普森以笔名普迪南姆威尔写的《有欠谨慎的北京来信》（中译作《庚子使馆被围记》）里记述说“5月31日洋兵武装进城”——第一批使馆卫队驻进使馆区，“6月4日拳民始由哈达门（今崇文门）进城。”——4天后，清政府才下决心向大队义和团打开城门。

北京街头的义和团民。

British journalist Bertram Lenox Simpson, who had witnessed the 1900 event, wrote *Indiscreet Letters from Peking* under the pseudonym of Putnam Weale. According to the book, armed foreign troops entered the City of Beijing on May 31—the first batch of legation guards stationed in the legation quarters. Four days later on June 4, the Boxers began to enter the City of Beijing from Hada Gate (today's Chongwen Gate), and the Qing Government opened the city gate to the principal force of the Boxers.

Boxers on a street in Beijing.

克林德(1853-1900)德国人，男爵。1899年任驻华公使。1900年6月19日，他得知英国海军中将西摩尔已率2000联军士兵自天津开向北京，“帮助清政府平叛”，就率卫队闯出使馆区，与各使馆卫队一起，连日逐杀义和团民。数天后，另一支联军攻下天津东南的大沽炮台，清政府闻讯于6月19日照会列强使馆“限二十四钟内，各国一切人等均须离京。”各公使不予理会。20日克林德外出与政府军发生冲突，中弹而亡。

German Baron von Ketteler (1853-1900) was appointed envoy to China in 1899. On June 19, 1900, after being informed that British Vice Admiral Seymour was leading 2,000 soldiers of the Allied Forces to Beijing from Tianjin "to help the Qing Government with the suppression," he took guards out of the legation quarters to work with guards of other legations in searching for Boxers. Days later, a branch of the Allied Forces captured Dagu Fort in southeast Tianjin. On June 19, the Qing Government notified all legations of the powers that "all foreigners must get out of Beijing within 24 hours." But the envoys took no notice. On June 20, Ketteler was shot dead in a conflict with government forces.

6月21日，清政府向列强宣战。日本学者山口一之认为“导致清政府宣战的原因，在于列强三项活动：一、调派使馆卫队进京。二、西摩尔联军北犯。三、攻击大沽炮台。

图为奉命攻打列强驻华使馆区的清政府军。

On June 21, the Qing Government declared war on the powers. According to a Japanese scholar, three activities of the powers attributed to the Qing Government's declaration of war: (1) moving legation guards to Beijing; (2) the northward advancement of Allied Forces led by Seymour; and (3) the attack of Dagu Fort.

Here are Qing government forces instructed to attack the legation quarters.

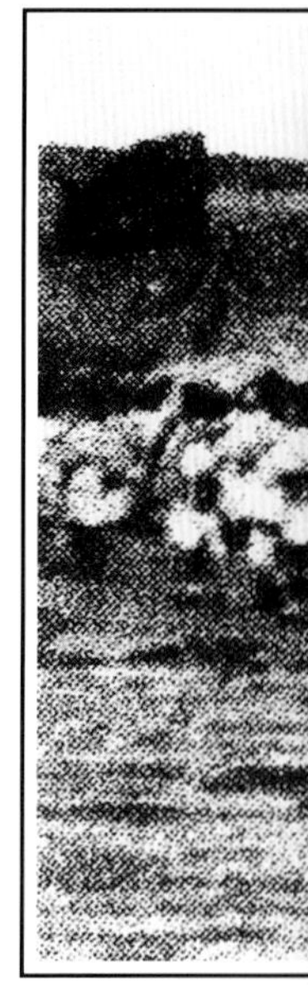

1900年6月16日晚，义和团认为正向北京进犯的西摩尔洋兵系该堂主教樊国梁所请，开始攻打西什库教堂，摧毁了教堂外围的部分建筑，未进教堂院内。

On the evening of June 16, 1900, the Boxers began to attack Pehtang Cathedral because they thought the foreign troops advancing toward Beijing, led by Seymour, were invited by Bishop Favier of the cathedral. They destroyed part of the peripheral buildings of the cathedral but failed to enter its courtyard.

▶ 英国公使馆卫队向清政府军和义和团开炮
Guards of the British legation fired at Qin government forces and Boxers.

参加围攻使馆的义和团团民和清政府军士兵。
Boxers and government soldiers who besieged the legations

▼ 使馆卫队在东交民巷巷口抵挡进攻的义和团团民与清政府军。

Legation guards resisted the attacking Boxers and government forces at the entrance into the lane of Dongjiaominxiang.

法国公使毕盛身背猎枪守卫使馆。

The French envoy, carrying his shotgun, defending the legation

赫德的办公地——邻近东交民巷的海关总税务司衙门被义和团攻毁。

The General Taxation Bureau of Customs near Dongjiaominxiang, with Robert Hart's office, was destroyed by the Boxers.

荣禄（1836 – 1903）大学士、军机大臣、兵部尚书、武卫军总统领，与西什库教堂樊国梁神甫通好。1900年6月21日，清政府向列强宣战，仅仅5天，又下令停攻使馆并加兵保护，继而又向使馆、教堂送瓜果、米面，均持荣禄令箭。

Rong Lu (1836-1903), Grand Secretary, Minister of Defense, Minister of War, and Commander-in-Chief of the Defense Army, maintained a good personal relationship with Father Favier of Pehtang Cathedral. The Qing Government declared war on the foreign powers on June 21, 1900, but five days later, it ordered a halt to the attack on the legations and sent forces to protect them. Fruit, rice and flour were sent to legations and churches under Rong's instructions.

First Setback

联军首败与占领天津

f the Allied Forces and the Capture of Tianjin

1900年6月10日，列强决定英国海军中将西摩尔出任联军统帅，率领英、法、俄、德、日、美、意等八国官兵2000人犯北京。在义和团与清政府军的协力阻击下，西摩尔联军进犯北京失败，退回天津。此时，联军攻取了天津的东大门——大沽炮台。于是，清军与联军发生大规模战事，战斗进行了二十余天，7月14日联军攻占天津，灾难降临在天津百姓头上。

On June 10, 1900, the allied powers decided to appoint British Vice Admiral Seymour as commander-in-chief of the Allied Forces, to lead an army of 2,000 soldiers of Britain, France, Russia, Germany, Japan, the United States and Italy, to invade Beijing. In face of the concerted resistance of the Boxers and Qing government forces, Seymour's army was defeated and retreated to Tianjin. The Allied Forces captured Dagu Fort, the eastern gate of Tianjin. Qing troops were engaged in a large-scale battle with the Allied Forces, which lasted for more than 20 days. On July 14, the Allied Forces occupied Tianjin, and calamity befell the people of Tianjin.

西摩尔(1840 – 1929)，英国远东舰队司令，海军中将。经八国联军及列强驻天津领事授权，西摩尔于1900年6月10日凌晨，率2000兵力自塘沽下舰，兵锋直指北京，对中国不宣而战。

Edward Hobart Seymour (1840-1929), vice admiral and commander-in-chief of the British Far East Fleet. At the authorization of the Eight-Power Allied Forces and the consuls of the powers in Tianjin, Seymour led an army of 2,000 that landed at Tanggu, Tianjin, to advance toward Beijing in the morning of June 10, 1900, thus launching a war against China without declaration.

联军携有机枪、火炮等重型武器，分乘5列火车向北京开进。
The Allied Forces, equipped with heavy weapons, such as machine guns and artillery, advanced toward Beijing aboard five trains.

西摩尔联军携带的地图上，标明了塘沽至北京的铁路及各车站站名。
The map used by the Allied Forces led by Seymour was marked with the railway from Tanggu to Beijing, as well as names of all the stations.

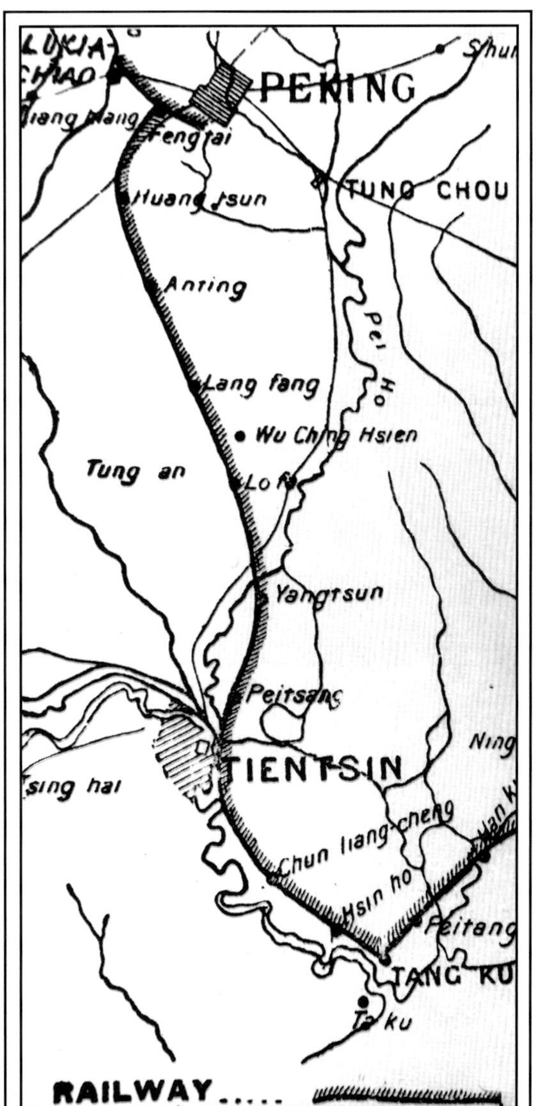

6月12日，行程近半的联军在廊坊遇到义和团和清政府军的阻击，被迫退回距天津30多公里的杨村车站，筑垒防守。

On June 12, the Allied Forces encountered the Boxers and Qing government forces at Langfang, halfway from Beijing. They had to retreat to Yangcun Station, more than 30 kilometers from Tianjin, to build their defenses.

义和团和清政府军破坏了铁路、桥梁，迫使西摩尔联军弃车，经北运河撤往天津。沿途，联军处处遭到攻击，历经半月，西摩尔才在援军的接应下，于6月26日率败兵撤入天津租界。此役历时17天，联军伤亡近300人。

The Boxers and Qing government forces destroyed the railway and bridges, which forced the Allied Forces, led by Seymour, to give up advancing by train and to retreat to Tianjin via the Northern Canal. The Allied Forces were constantly attacked all the way. After 15 days of hard struggle, Seymour and his defeated troops retreated to the concession in Tianjin, with the aid of reinforcements, on June 26. This battle lasted for 17 days and there were approximately 300 casualties on the side of the Allied Forces.

阿列克谢耶夫（1843 – 1909）俄国太平洋舰队司令，1900年六、七月间曾代替西摩尔行使联军总指挥的权力。6月17日，他命令俄、英、美、日、德、意等多国战舰和海军陆战队，攻占清政府屏护天津的军事要塞——大沽炮台。此后，又指挥了联军攻打天津。

Alexeyev (1843-1909), commander-in-chief of the Russian Pacific Fleet, assumed the power as commander-in-chief of the Allied Forces in June and July 1900. On June 17, he ordered the warships and marine corps of Russia, Britain, the United States, Japan, Germany and Italy to attack and capture Dagu Fort, the military fortress of the Qing Government for the defense of Tianjin. After that, he directed the attack of Tianjin by the Allied Forces.

大沽炮台紧把海河入海口两岸，南北各设两座炮台，装备火炮170门，是联军向津、京用兵登陆的最大障碍。还在四、五月份，列强的军舰就已云集大沽口外的海面，随时准备向炮台动武。6月17日凌晨，为配合西摩尔联军进攻北京，列强向炮台下最后通牒，要求守军无条件投降。守军不从，各舰立即开炮。

这一通牒和开炮，导致北京使馆区被围困、被攻打。当时，美国传教士明恩溥就说："是最后通牒，相应导致了限定使馆24小时内撤出北京的命令。"

Dagu Fort was located at the estuary of the Haihe River. With one battery in the north and south respectively, it was equipped with 170 cannons. It was the biggest obstacle for the landing of the Allied Forces before they could launch a military attack on Tianjin and Beijing. Earlier, in April and May, the allied powers' warships had gathered at sea near Dagu Fort, preparing for a military attack on the fort. In the early morning of June 17, as a coordination of Seymour's attack on Beijing, the allied powers issued an ultimatum to the battery, demanding an unconditional surrender of Chinese soldiers. As the defending Chinese soldiers refused the request, the warships immediately fired cannons.

The ultimatum and attack led to the siege and attack of the legation quarters in Beijing. Arthur Henderson Smith, an American missionary, said, "It is the ultimatum that led to the order that legations should withdraw from Beijing within 24 hours."

◀ 参战的美国军舰″马拉卡西″号
A US warship

▼ 参战的英国军舰森特隆号。
British warship *Centurlon* in the war

▼ 参战的法国军舰登特里卡斯特号。
French warship *D'Entrecasteau*

德国军舰伊尔蒂斯号。此舰中炮弹十数发，包括舰长，伤亡多人。
German warship *Yetis* was hit by dozens of shells and suffered heavy casualties, including its captain.

日本军舰富士号参加了进攻。
Japanese warship *Fuji* participated in a military operation.

俄国军舰基略克号。此舰被重创，弹药库中炮引爆，被迫退出战场。
This Russian warship was severely damaged. As its ammunition stores exploded after being hit by shells, it was forced to pull out of the battle.

大沽炮台被联军炮火彻底摧毁，守军阵亡千余人。
Dagu Fort was completely destroyed under the attack of the Allied Forces. More than 1,000 Chinese soldiers were killed in action.

日军首先攻占了西北炮台。
Japanese troops were the first to capture the northwestern battery.

大沽炮台废墟上的美日士兵。
US and Japanese soldiers on the ruins of Dagu Fort

聂士成，直隶提督，清政府军著名将领。1894年中日战争期间，曾在辽东战场击毙日将富冈三造．所部采用德国的武器和训练方法，是清政府守卫天津的主力。大沽炮台失陷当日，聂率部与义和团围攻租界。不久，移师八里台，7月9日，死于阵前。

Nie Shicheng, Commander-in-Chief of Zhili Province, was a renowned leading officer of the Qing government forces. During the Sino-Japanese War in 1894, he killed a Japanese general, Sanzo Tomioka, on the Liaodong battlefield. The troops under his leadership, using German weapons and training methods, were the main forces of the Qing Government for defending Tianjin. The day Dagu Fort fell, Nie's troops, together with the Boxers, laid a siege to the concession. Shortly afterwards, Nie moved his men to Balitai and was killed in action on July 9.

这是法租界被聂军炮火扫过的一角。

Part of the French concession after the attack by Nie's troops

租界对面的老龙头火车站是连接京津二地的要冲，在天津攻守战中，化作断壁残垣。

Laolongtou Railway Station, opposite the concession, was a strategic point connecting Beijing and Tianjin. It was reduced to rubble in the Tianjin battle.

天津机器局东局——清政府在华北最大的军火工厂。6月27日，被联军攻下，截断了清政府军的弹药补给。

The Eastern Division of the Tianjin Machinery Bureau, the largest armament plant of the Qing Government in north China. On June 27, it fell into the hands of the Allied Forces and the ammunition supply of the Chinese government forces was cut off.

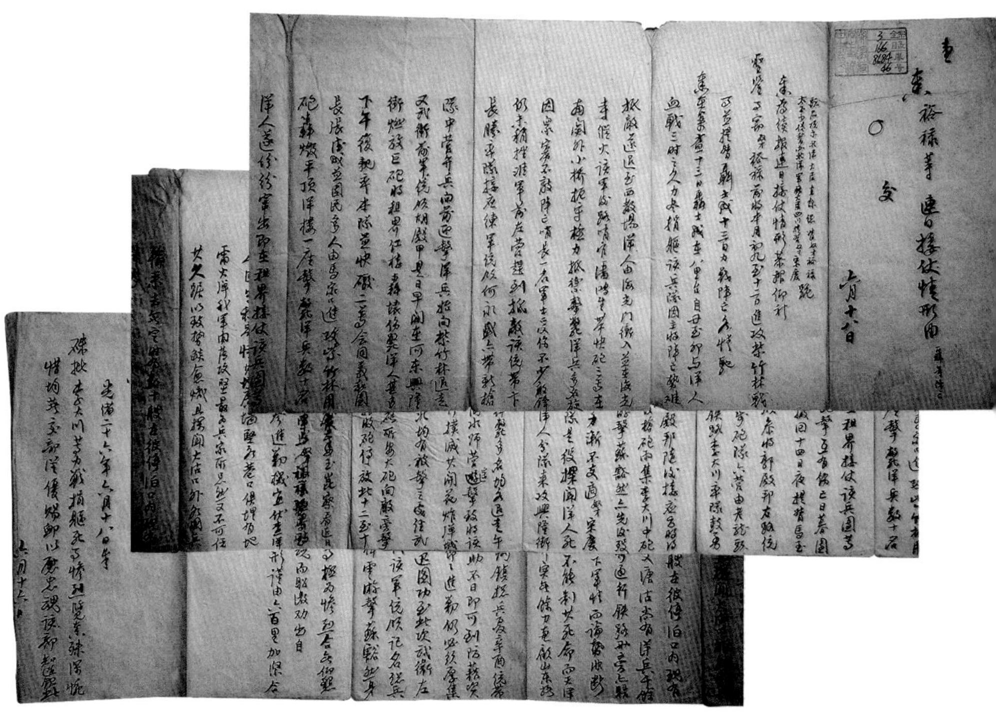

1900年7月14日，直隶总督裕禄向清政府汇报天津战况的奏折。

On July 14, 1900, Yu Lu, Governor-General of Zhili, reported to the Qing Government the situation in Tianjin in this memorial to the throne.

兵力已拥有优势的联军，移动炮位，准备轰击天津。
The artilleries of the Allied Forces ready to attack Tianjin

联军炮击天津城。
The Allied Forces firing cannons at the City of Tianjin

被联军炮火摧毁的天津南门城楼。
The southern gate tower of Tianjin destroyed by artillery fire of the Allied Forces

9月14日，联军从这里攻入天津城。
On September 14, the Allied Forces forced their way into the City of Tianjin.

攻破天津海光门（也称南营门）后，联军中的英、日军士兵正做片刻喘息。

British and Japanese soldiers in the Allied Forces taking a break after breaching Tianjin's Haiguang Gate (also called Nanying Gate).

战死的守城者。
Chinese soldiers killed defending the city

联军炮击后的城内民房。
A residential building in the city after the artillery attack by the Allied Forces

法国机枪小分队开进天津城。
The French machine gun squad marching into the City of Tianjin

参加攻打天津城的德军军官入城后合影。
German officers participating in the attack of Tianjin taking a group photo after getting into the city

天津城破之后，联军万余官兵整整抢劫了一天。清政府财政机构、当铺和商号首当其冲。仅长芦盐运使衙门（负责盐税机构）一处，日军就掠去白银200万两。美军从这里掠获的存银也有几百万两，图为被挖掘出来的银锭堆成小山。
After the fall of Tianjin, more than 10,000 foreign officers and soldiers looted for an entire day. Financial institutions of the government, pawnshops and business firms were the first to suffer. From the Changlu Office of Salt in charge of salt taxation, Japanese troops plundered 2 million taels of silver. The Americans also looted the place of several million taels of silver. The picture shows heaps of unearthed silver ingots.

中国百姓的耕牛很快就会在联军行军锅里煎成牛排。
Chinese people's cattle would soon become steaks in the field caldrons of the Allied Forces.

7月30日，俄海军中将阿列克谢耶夫提议，俄、日、英三国各派一名校官组成治理天津的三人"临时政府"——中国人称之为"天津都统衙门。11月，美、法、德也各派一军人加入都统衙门，组成六人委员会，共同管理天津。

On July 30, Russian Vice Admiral Alexeyev proposed that Russia, Japan and Britain each appoint a field officer to form a three-member "provisional government," which the Chinese called the "Tientsin Provisional Government." In November, the United States, France and Germany also dispatched one military officer each to join the "provisional government" and form a six-member committee to govern Tianjin.

坐镇天津都统衙门的这些军人既拥有立法权、司法权，又握有行政权。清政府直隶总督李鸿章上任，也得向这些上校、中校们通报。

Military officers that assumed personal command in the Tientsin Provisional Government possessed not only legislative and judicial power, but also executive power. Even when Governor-General of Zhili Li Hongzhang took up his office, he had to report to these military officers.

对怀疑是义和团民的人，无须经过必要的司法程序，即在街头斩首。

Anyone suspected of being a Boxer would be executed on the street without going through necessary judicial procedures.

都统衙门借助中外巡捕、军队的支持，大规模地捕杀团民及被怀疑是义和团的同情者。

With the help of Chinese and foreign police and military forces, the Provisional Government hunted the Boxers and all those suspected of sympathizing with them.

联军攻占天津城后，举行了大规模阅兵式。英军赶往阅兵场。那个背对画外的人是都统衙门维持秩序的华人巡捕。
The Allied Forces held a large-scale parade after they captured Tianjin. The picture shows British troops on their way to the parade ground. The person with his back towards the camera was a Chinese policeman in the Provisional Government for maintaining order.

▼联军列队欢迎租界的领事。
The Allied Forces line up to welcome the consuls in the concessions.

▲ 阅兵式队列之一。
One of the formations in the parade

◀ 阅兵式队列之一。
One of the formations in the parade

阅兵式队列之二。
Another formation in the parade

阅兵后，联军军官们合影。
A group photo of officers of the Allied Forces after the parade

天津城遭联军炮火破坏严重，直到冬季来临，天津还处处可以看到荒凉惨状。

The City of Tianjin was severely damaged by artillery fire of the Allied Forces. Everywhere in Tianjin was a scene of desolation at the advent of winter.

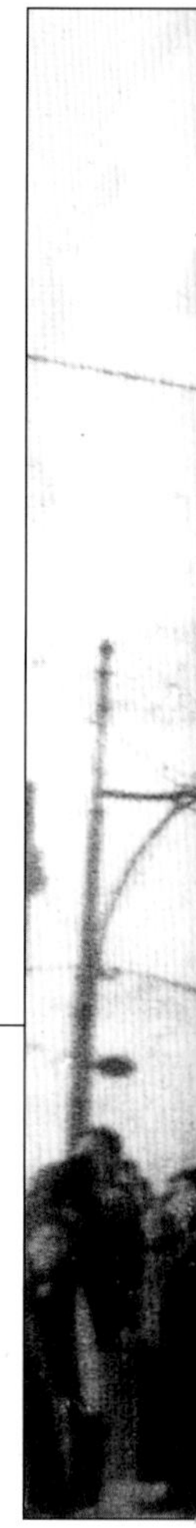

残破街景之一
Here is a street scene after the capture.

残破街景之二
Another street scene

The

八国联军攻占北京

ure of Beijing by the Eight-Power Allied Forces

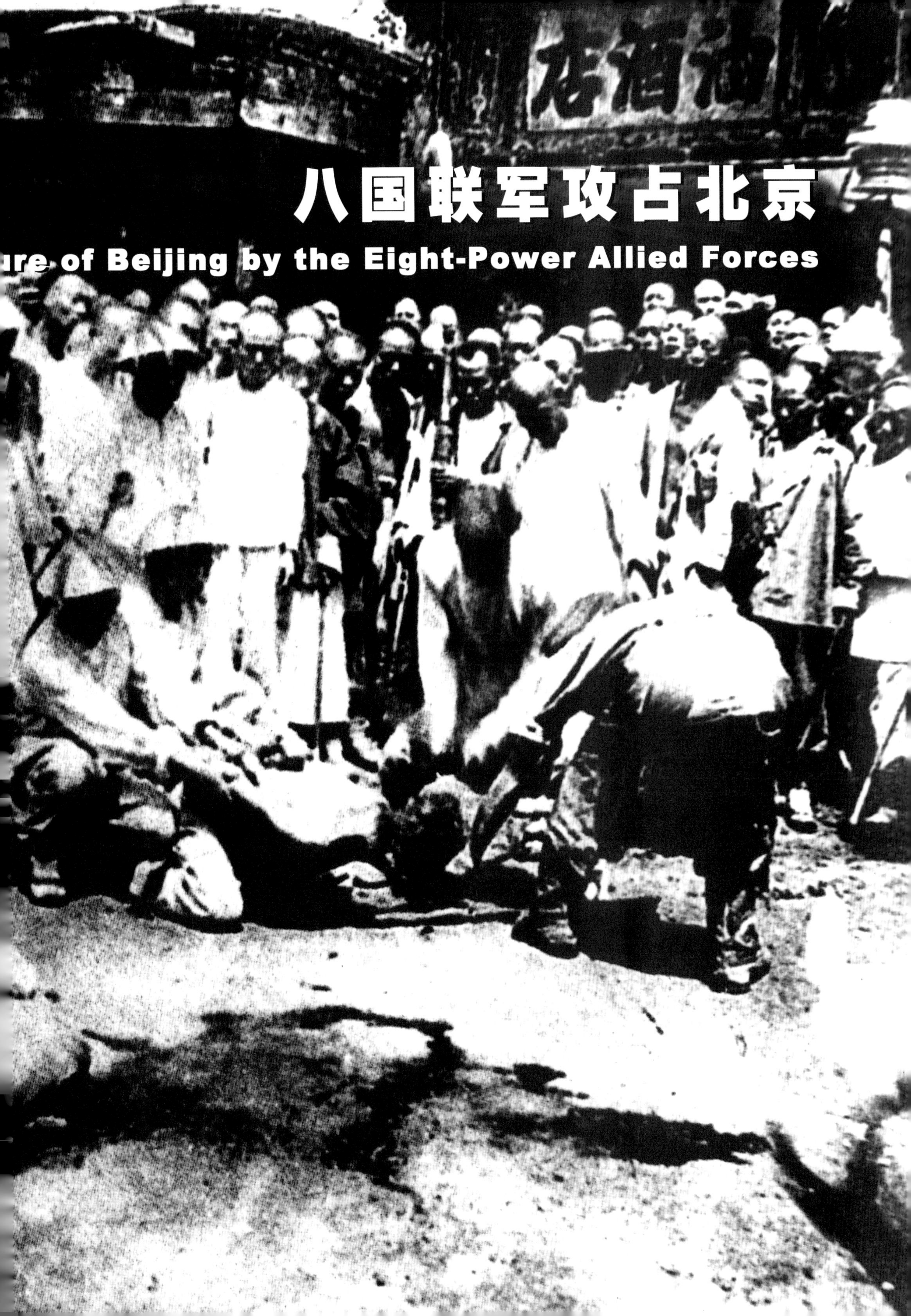

1900年8月4日，联军近2万人由天津出兵北京，一路突破清政府军的抵抗，于14日攻进北京城内。联军入城后，杀戮、抢劫、强奸层出不穷。法国人贝野罗蒂回国后出版了《北京的末日》，写道："城里的寂寞和荒凉，也正和城外一样，除了残毁、残毁、残毁之外，是再没有其他的东西了……一座昔日充满着辉煌房舍的北京城，现在是一片荒野。"

On August 4, 1900, approximately 20,000 Allied Forces marched toward Beijing from Tianjin. They defeated the Chinese troops in succession and captured Beijing on August 14. After they entered the city, the Allied Forces plunged into a massacre. There were countless occurrences of bloodshed, looting and rape. A Frenchman published a book entitled *The End of Peking* after he returned to France. He wrote: "The solitude and desolation were the same in and outside the city. There was nothing except rubble everywhere....The city of Peking, which was full of splendid buildings in the past, is now a wilderness."

从大沽登陆的军队和战争物资不断运抵天津火车站，联军向北京进兵的时间已进入倒计时。

Troops and war materials landing at Dagu and being transported to Tianjin Railway Station. The time for the Allied Forces to march toward Beijing was drawing nearer.

联军决定，8月4日进攻北京。这是联军的司令官们离津前的最后一张合影。

The Allied Forces decided to attack Beijing on August 4. This is the last group photo of the commanders of the Allied Forces before departing from Tianjin.

8月3日，联军中的英军军官出发前，在天津合影留念。

British officers in the Allied Forces took a group photo in Tianjin on August 3 before the departure.

向北京进发的联军，包括美国第15步兵团的这支乐队。
The Allied Forces marching to Beijing included this band of the 15th US infantry regiment.

行进中的联军的炮车。
Artillery prime movers of the Allied Forces in the advancement

联军中的英军指挥官在前线视察。

British officers inspecting the frontline

沿运河行进的联军，突破清政府布设的北仓防线。1000多名政府军士兵遗尸战场。
The Allied Forces marching along the canal broke through the Qing government line of defense at Beicang. More than 1,000 government soldiers were killed on the battlefield.

8月6日，联军攻破杨村防线，缴获清政府军帅旗。政府军统帅、直隶总督裕禄自杀。
On August 6, the Allied Forces breached the line of defense at Yangcun and captured the commanding banner of the Qing forces. Yu Lu, commander-in-chief of the government forces and Governor-General of Zhili, committed suicide.

津京间的平原，无险可守。联军中的英军威尔士营突入京郊。

The plains between Tianjin and Beijing were strategically indefensible. The British Welsh Battalion charged into suburban Beijing.

突破清政府军在京郊又一道防线后，联军电讯车随司令部启程前移。三年前，无线电通讯刚刚被意大利人马可尼发明，现在就武装了部队。

After breaching another line of defense deployed by the Qing Government in suburban Beijing, telecommunication vehicles of the Allied Forces moved forward with the headquarters. Radio communication, which had been invented by Italian Guglielmo Marconi three years before, was used to arm the Allied Forces.

联军占领距北京20多公里的通县。
The Allied Forces occupied Tongxian County, more than 20 kilometers from Beijing.

8月11日，联军突破清政府在京郊的最后防线，政府军马玉崑提督、张春发总兵的军旗落入敌手。

On August 11, the Allied Forces breached the last line of defense of the Qing Government in suburban Beijing. The banners of Ma Yukun and Zhang Chunfa, two high-ranking military officers, fell into the hands of the enemy.

驻守通州的联军加紧练兵，准备进攻北京城。

The Allied Forces stationed in Tongzhou intensified training in preparation for the attack on the City of Beijing.

山口素臣中将，侵华日军司令官，参加过1894年中日战争，以冷酷、残忍著称。1900年7月，自广岛率13000日军来华，充任联军主力。

Lieutenant General Mototomi Yamaguchi was commander-in-chief of the Japanese troops invading China. He participated in the Sino-Japanese War in 1894 and was known for his cruelty. In July 1900, he led 13,000 Japanese troops from Hiroshima to China, to serve as a main force of the allied troops.

▲ 8月13日联军下令进攻北京城，通州的日军整装待发。
On August 13, the Allied Forces started to attack the City of Beijing. The Japanese troops in Tongzhou were ready and waiting for their departure orders.

英军开出通州营房。
British troops leave the barracks.

法军同大部分俄军策马出营。
The French troops and the majority of the Russian troops spur their horses out of their barracks.

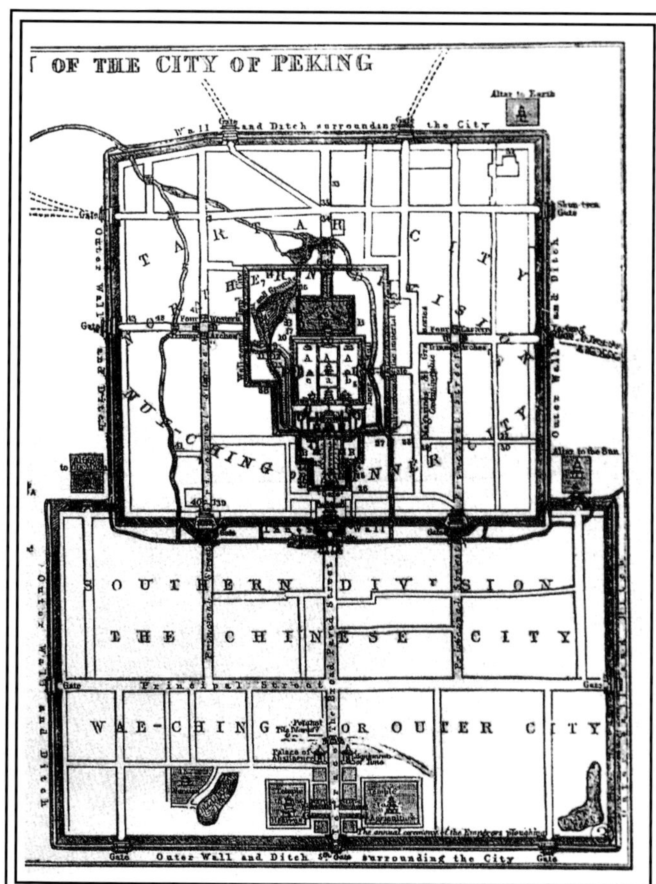

联军用的北京地图。古城被描画的十分清楚，格局为城城相套 — 紫禁城（宫城）被皇城围住，皇城又被京城围住。借京城南墙作北墙，又接出去一座城池，这座城习惯上被称为北京的外城，与其相接的京城部分则称内城。
The map of Beijing used by the Allied Forces. The composition of "city within city" of ancient Beijing was vividly depicted. The Forbidden City (Imperial Palace) was in the Tartar City, which was in the Chinese City. The southern wall of the Chinese City was taken as the northern wall of another city, which was called the Outer City, while the part adjoining the Outer City was called the Inner City.

董福祥（1840 – 1908）甘肃提督，义和团起事前，即奉命率甘军11000人入京，充任武卫后军，守护京师。他及所部官兵，对义和团持同情态度，参与了围攻使馆区和教堂的战斗。在北京攻防战中，他负责防守从东直门到广渠门的整个东线，独挡联军的正面进攻。

Dong Fuxiang (1840-1908) was Commander-in- Chief of Gansu Province. Before the outbreak of the Boxer Uprising, he was instructed to lead 11,000 Gansu troops to protect Beijing. His troops, being sympathizers of the Boxers, participated in the siege of the legation quarters and churches. In the battle to defend Beijing, he was responsible for resisting the Allied Forces in the entire eastern line from Dongzhimen to Guangqumen.

8月13日下午，联军参加攻城的13700人，赶到各自的进攻出发地。日军被分配攻打朝阳门、东直门和安定门。这是日军在列阵。
In the afternoon of August 13, the 13,700-strong Allied Forces waited at their respective places for the attack. The Japanese troops were assigned to attack Chaoyangmen, Dongzhimen and Andingmen. Pictured here are the Japanese formations.

一队日本工兵即将参加进攻东直门。
These Japanese engineers are ready for the attack of Dongzhimen.

8月14日凌晨，俄法联军用大炮向东便门抵近射击，揭开了联军攻城的序幕。东便门的箭楼被炸得面目全非。

In the early morning of August 14, the Russian and French troops fired at Dongbianmen with cannons, raising the curtain of the attack on the City of Beijing. The watchtower over the city gate at Dongbianmen was damaged beyond recognition.

日军集中几十门大炮，轰击朝阳门，摧毁箭楼，攻入城内，并向东直门，安定门方向，扩大战果。清政府10万守兵溃散。

Japanese troops bombarded at Chaoyangmen with dozens of cannons. They destroyed the watchtower and flooded into the city, heading for Dongzhimen and Andingmen. The 100,000 Qing government forces defending the city collapsed in disorder.

由于守军疏漏，参战的美军士兵，从古都东南一段城墙攀援而上，撕开了守军防线。
US soldiers climbed onto a section of the southeastern city wall, breaching the line of defense.

英军自广渠门攻进外城，又从外城、内城间找到图上这一泄水口，潜入内城，最先进入使馆区。
British troops forced their way into the Outer City from Guangqumen and found this opening for water drainage, as shown in the picture, between the Outer City and the Inner City. They sneaked into the Inner City and became the first to enter into the legation quarters.

英军士兵和两个教民在解围后的英国公使馆墙外。
A British soldier and two Chinese Christians outside the wall of the British legation after the rescue

美军攻入内城。用大炮轰开大清门、天安门的包铁巨门，列阵紫禁城下。此前几小时，慈禧太后携光绪皇帝仓惶辞宫，自德胜门出城，逃往西安。

远处箭头所示建筑即为大清门。

The US troops entered the Inner City after they forced open the giant iron-covered doors at the gates of Daqingmen and Tian'anmen. A few hours earlier, Empress Dowager Cixi and Emperor Guangxu rushed out of the palace. They left the city from Deshengmen and fled to Xi'an.

The structure in the distance marked with an arrow is Daqingmen.

被联军炮火摧毁的商业街。
A business street destroyed by artilleries of the Allied Forces

占领北京后，为彻底消灭义和团，联军频繁会晤。这是各国军队的指挥官，在日军司令部议事后合影。

After the capture of Beijing, to completely eliminate the Boxers, the Allied Forces met frequently. Here is a group photo of commanders of different nations at the Japanese headquarters after an official discussion.

联军攻入城后，义和团和部分政府军仍在进行抵抗。于是，联军在北海施放载人气球，进行高空侦察。
Despite the entry of the Allied Forces, the Boxers and some government forces continued their resistance. The Allied Forces then hoisted a manned balloon in Beihai to conduct reconnaissance from the air.

联军对捕获的义和团或怀疑是义和团的人立即处决。联军统帅瓦德西承认说：“由此而死之人究有若干，实永远不能查清。”（见《瓦德西回忆录》）

The Allied Forces promptly put to death all captured Boxers, or those suspected of being Boxers. Waldersee, commander-in-chief of the Allied Forces, admitted: "Nobody knew how many people were put to death as Boxers." (See *Memoirs of Waldersee*)

听命于联军的巡捕将义和团团民押往刑场。

Police dancing to the pipe of the Allied Forces escorting Boxers to the execution ground

联军派代表监督处斩团民。
Boxers were executed under supervision of representatives of the Allied Forces.

联军进城之初，这个街头刑场天天杀人。

In the first days after the Allied Forces entered the city, this street execution ground witnessed killing day after day.

日军在辖区的安定门外设刑场，斩杀中国人。
The Japanese troops set up an execution ground for killing Chinese outside the gate of Andingmen, which was under its control.

受刑者暴尸街头。
The corpse of an executed person on the street

联军统帅瓦德西在回忆录中写道："联军占领北京后，曾特许军队公开抢劫三日"。联军抢劫，无所顾忌。这是被日军烧毁前的清政府户部衙门。日军在此处掠走300万两存银，继之举火灭迹。

Waldersee, commander-in-chief of the Allied Forces, wrote in his memoirs, "After the Allied Forces captured Beijing, they were given special permission for open plunder." The Allied Forces went all lengths in their pillage. Pictured here is the seat of the Qing Government's Ministry of Revenue before it was burnt down by Japanese troops. The Japanese took 3 million taels of silver from here before setting it on fire.

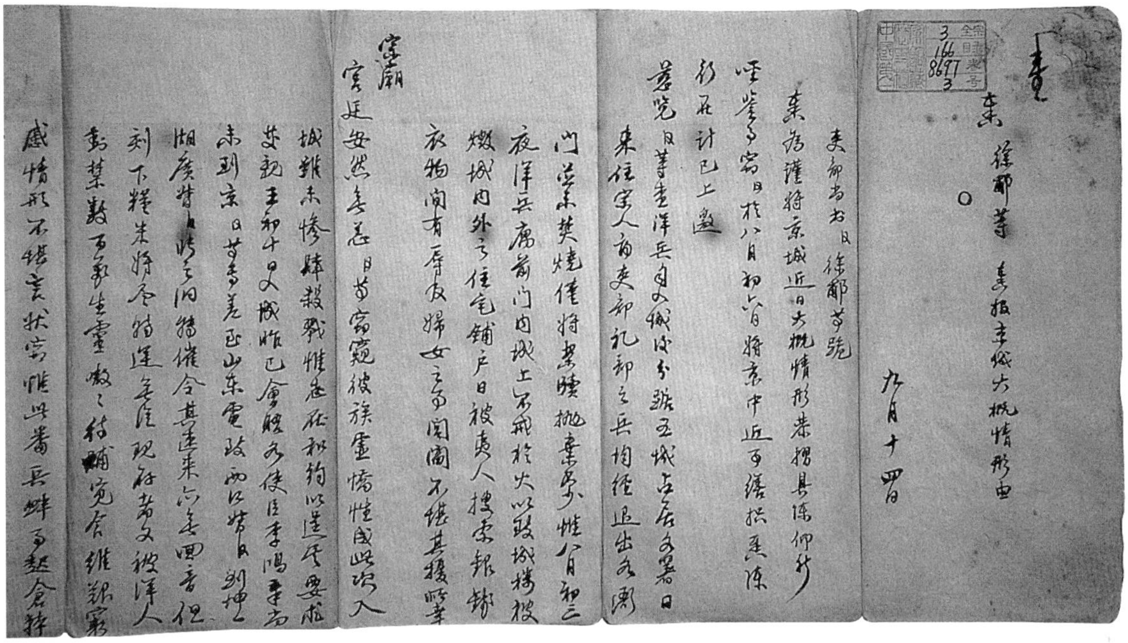

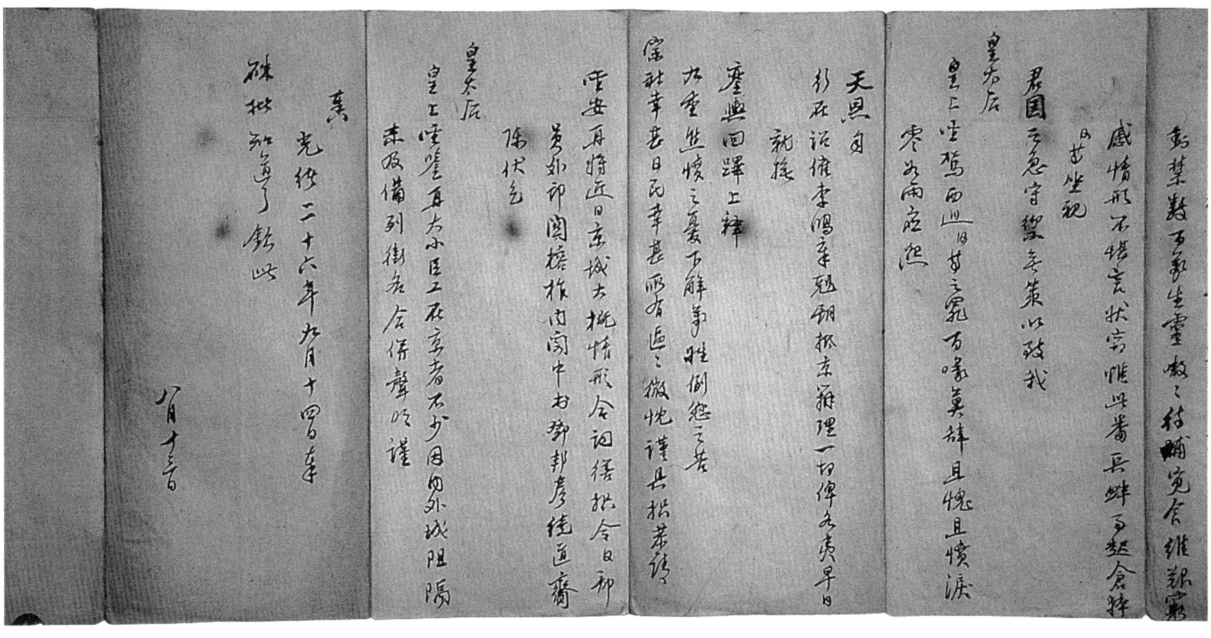

1900年9月6日，吏部尚书徐郙等奏报洋兵入京掠抢及污辱妇女情形的录副奏折。

A copy of the memorial to the throne, presented by Xu Fu, Minister of Civil Personnel, and other officials on September 6, 1900, reporting on the plunder by foreign troops in Beijing and on Chinese women being raped by foreign soldiers

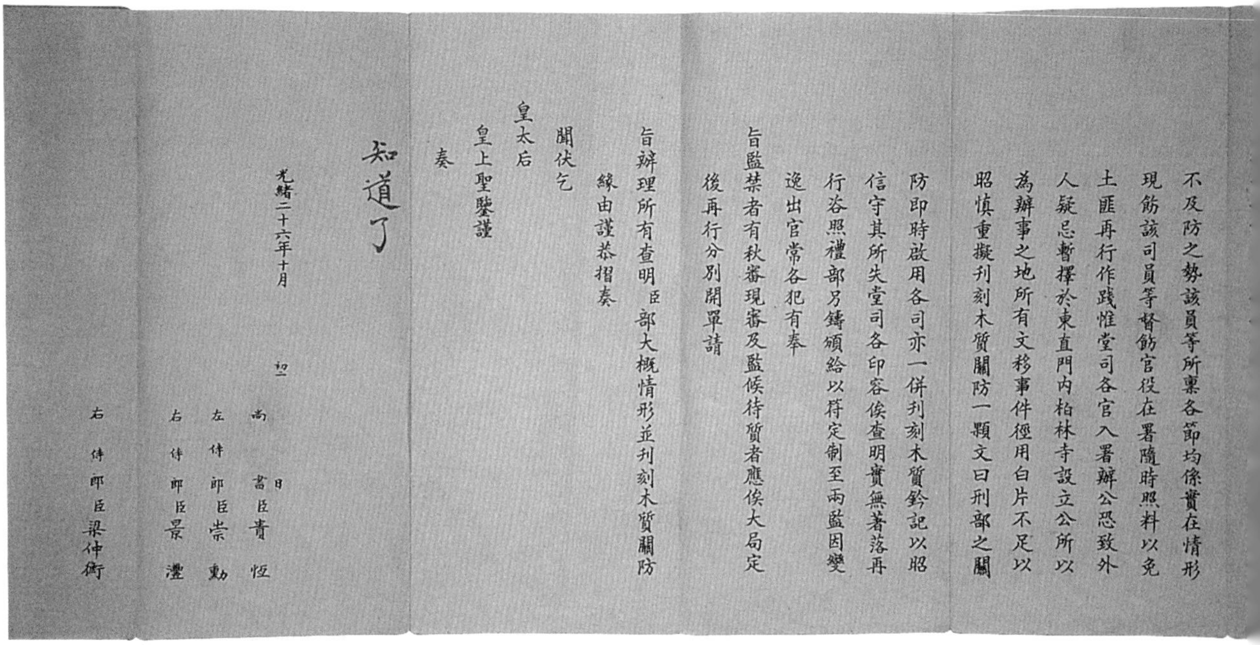

不及防之勢該員等所稟各節均係實在情形
現飭該司員等督飭官役在署隨時照料以免
土匪再行作踐惟堂司各官入署辦公恐致外
人疑忌暫擇於東直門內柏林寺設立公所以
為辦事之地所有文移事件徑用白片不足以
昭慎重擬刊刻木質關防一顆文曰刑部之關
防即時啟用各司亦一併刊刻木質鈐記以昭
信守其所失堂司各印容俟查明實無著落再
行咨照禮部另鑄頒給以符定制至兩監因變
逸出官常各犯有奉
旨監禁者有秋審現審及監候待質者應俟大局定
後再行分別開單請
旨辦理所有查明臣部大概情形並刊刻木質關防
緣由謹恭摺奏
聞伏乞
皇太后
皇上聖鑒謹
奏
知道了
光緒二十六年十月 初二 日
尚書臣貴恒
左侍郎臣崇勳
右侍郎臣景灃
右侍郎臣梁仲衡

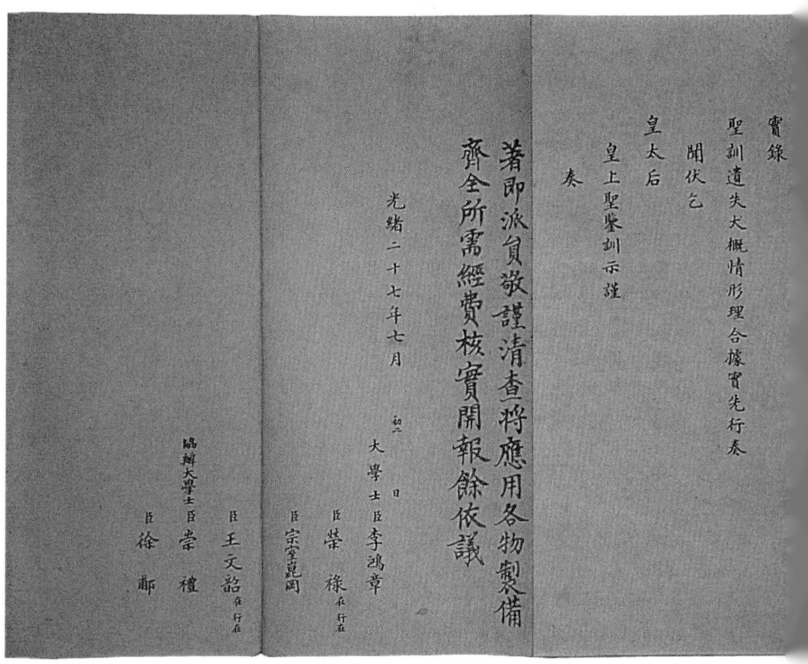

實錄
聖訓遺失大概情形理合據實先行奏
聞伏乞
皇太后
皇上聖鑒訓示謹
奏
著即派員敬謹清查將應用各物製備齊全所需經費核實開報餘依議
光緒二十七年七月 初二 日
大學士臣李鴻章
臣榮祿 在行在
臣宗室崑岡
臣王文韶 在行在
協辦大學士臣崇禮
臣徐郙

▶ 1901 年 8 月 16 日李鸿章向皇帝呈报皇史宬实录、圣训丢失的奏折。

The memorial to the throne presented by Li Hongzhang on August 16, 1901 about the loss of records and emperors' quotations in the Royal Archives

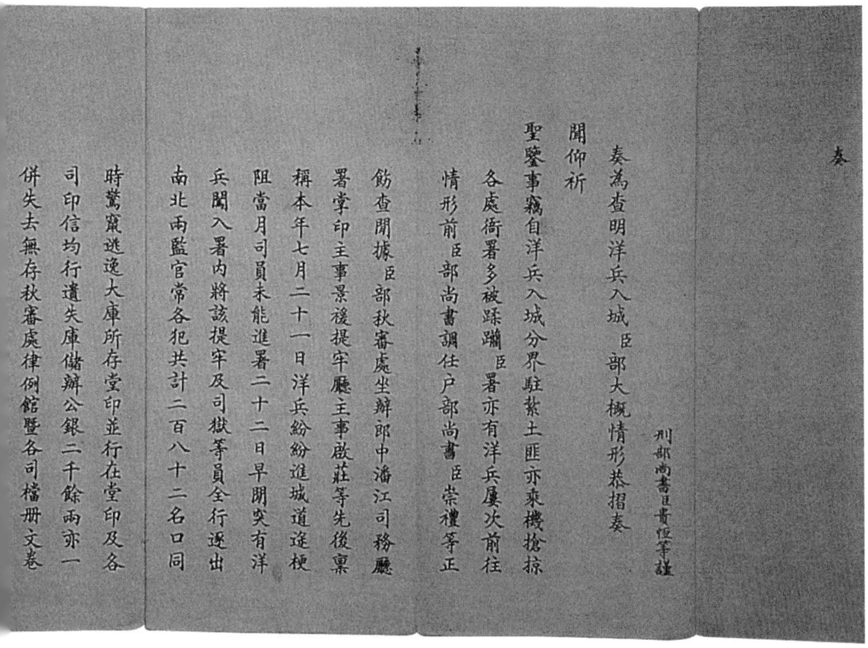

奏
刑部尚書臣貴恒等謹
奏為查明洋兵入城臣部大概情形恭摺奏
聞仰祈
聖鑒事竊自洋兵入城分界駐紮土匪亦乘機搶掠
各處衙署多被蹂躪臣署亦有洋兵屢次前往
情形前臣部尚書調任戶部尚書臣崇禮等正
飭查間據臣部秋審處坐辦郎中潘江司務廳
署掌印主事景襚提牢廳主事啟莊等先後稟
稱本年七月二十一日洋兵紛紛進城道途梗
阻當月司員未能進署二十二日早開突有洋
兵闖入署內將該提牢及司獄等員全行逐出
南北兩監官常各犯共計二百八十二名口同
時驚竄逃逸大庫所存堂印並行在堂印及各
司印信均行遺失庫儲辦公銀二千餘兩亦一
併失去無存秋審處律例館暨各司檔冊文卷

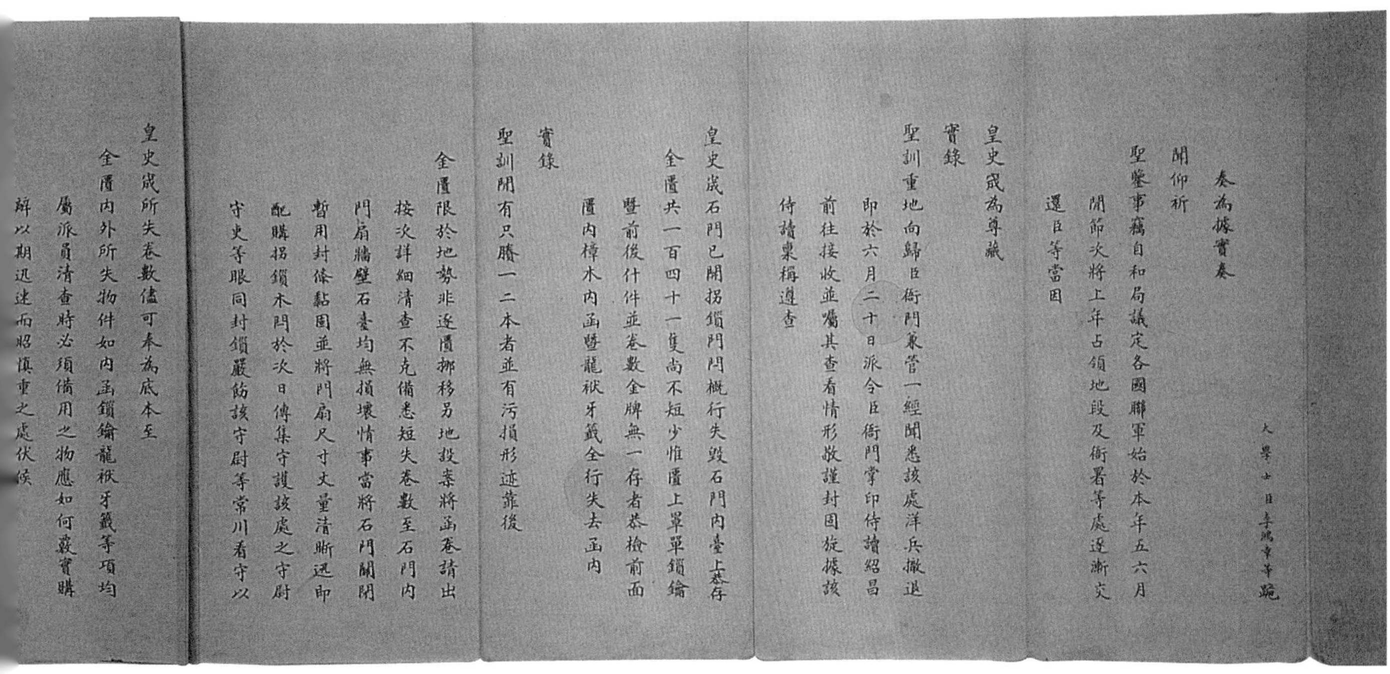

大學士臣李鴻章等跪
奏為據實奏
聞仰祈
聖鑒事竊自和局議定各國聯軍始於本年五六月
間節次將上年占領地段及衙署等處逐漸交
還臣等當因
皇史宬為尊藏
實錄
聖訓重地向歸臣衙門兼管一經聞悉該處洋兵撤退
即於六月二十日派令臣衙門掌印侍讀紹昌
前往接收並囑其查看情形敬謹封固旋據該
侍讀稟稱遵查
皇史宬石門已開拐鎖門閂概行失毀石門內臺上恭存
金匱共一百四十一隻尚不短少惟匱上罩單鎖鑰
暨前後什件並卷數金牌無一存者恭檢前面
匱內樟木內函暨龍袱牙籤全行失去函內
實錄
聖訓間有只賸一二本者並有污損形迹詳後
金匱限於地勢非逐匱挪移另地設案將函卷請出
按次詳細清查不克備悉短失卷數至石門內
門扇牆壁石臺均無損壞情事當將石門關閉
暫用封條黏固並將門扇尺寸丈量清晰迅即
配購拐鎖木閂於次日傳集守護該處之守尉
守吏等眼同封鎖嚴飭該守尉等常川看守以
皇史宬所失卷數儘可本為底本至
金匱內外所失物件如內函鎖鑰龍袱牙籤等項均
屬派員清查時必須備用之物應如何發實購
辦以期迅速而昭慎重之處伏候

◀ 1900年11月23日刑部尚书贵恒等向皇帝呈报洋兵进入北京城抢劫情况的奏折。

The memorial to the throne presented by Gui Heng, Minister of Justice, and other officials on the entry of foreign troops into the City of Beijing

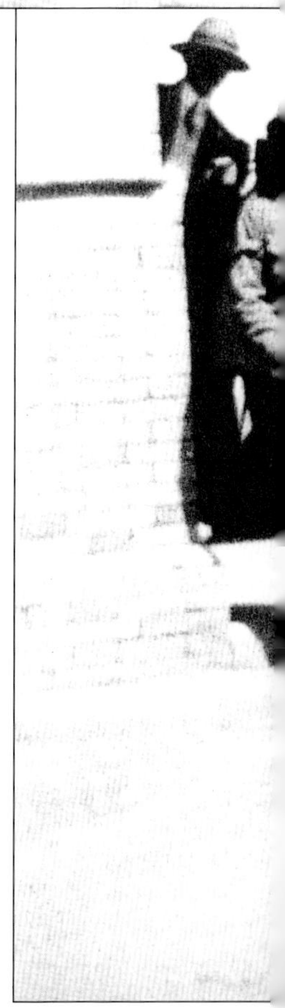

建于1442年的古观象台，设置于北京东城墙上，存放的天文仪器形质精美，有极高的应用和科学价值。联军中的德国人派兵拆卸，准备运走。

The ancient observatory, built in 1442 on the eastern city wall of Beijing, housed valuable astronomical instruments. The Germans were dismantling the instruments so they could take them away.

法军要求分享天文仪器，说有几件是法国皇帝送给中国前代皇帝的，要求"物归原主"。德国人让步，法国公使馆的人抱着这些"早已入籍中国"的仪器，摄影留念。
The French wanted a share of the astronomical instruments, saying that several articles were gifts from French emperors to previous Chinese emperors, and should "be restored to their original owner." The Germans gave in. People from the French legation carried these instruments, which had long been owned by the Chinese, to be photographed.

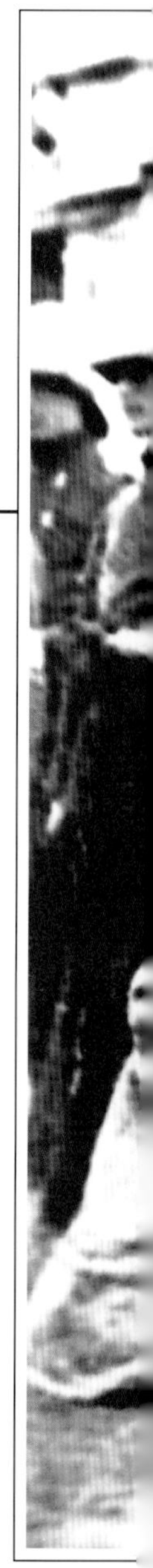

在中国皇帝敬天的神圣禁地 — 天坛驻军的英士兵，将掠来的东西胡乱堆放在殿檐下。
British soldiers piled up their loot under the eaves of the Temple of Heaven, a sacred place where Chinese emperors offered sacrifices to Heaven.

以搜捕义和团为借口，联军闯入修研藏传佛教的雍和宫，把喇嘛强行拘到一起。联军走后，喇嘛发现，大量的金银法器、佛像不翼而飞。

Under the pretext of searching for Boxers, the Allied Forces broke into the Yonghe Lamasery, which specialized in the practice of Tibetan Buddhism. After the Allied Forces left, the lamas at the temple found that much of their gold and silver musical instruments used for performing religious rites and Buddhist statues were gone.

当年美国《纽约先驱报》登载消息说，"曾任外交要职而反对排外运动被西太后免职的立山家属，控告樊国梁曾到其家行抢，劫去财物珍宝约一百万两（白银）。"樊神甫向《巴黎时报》承认，这次抢劫及他组织教徒的其他抢劫，是经法国驻华公使毕盛先生准许的。这是西什库教堂在清点抢来的金银珠宝。

The US *New York Herald* reported that the family of a dismissed Qing official complained that Favier had looted property and treasures worth 1 million taels of silver. Favier told the *Paris Times* that this and other plunder he organized had the permission of the French envoy to China. Here at Pehtang Cathedral, gold, silver and jewelry they had looted were being checked.

英军在外城天坛和内城西部驻军，这是西城的一处衙门被英军占驻。

British troops garrisoned at the Temple of Heaven in the Outer City and in the western part of the Inner City. The picture shows a Qing government office occupied by British troops.

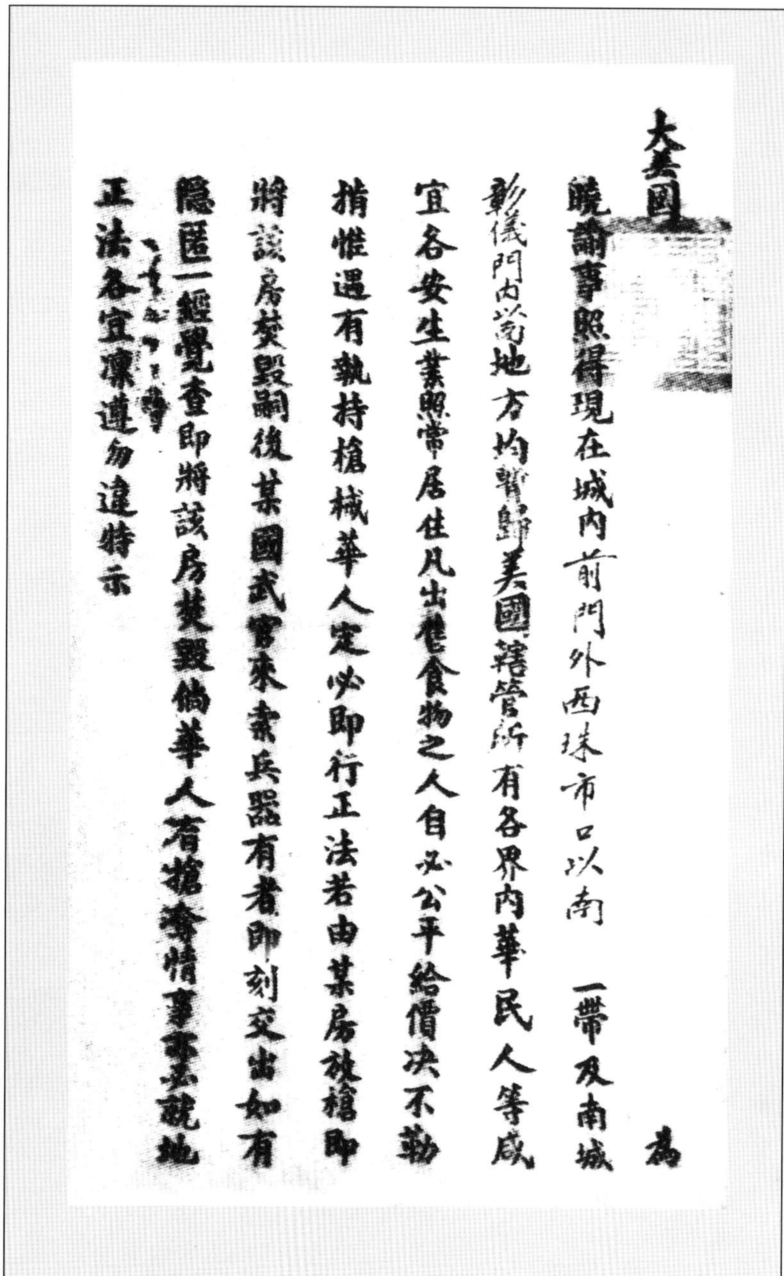
大美國
為
曉諭事照得現在城內前門外西珠市口以南 一帶及南城
彰儀門內並地方均暫歸美國管轄所有各界內華民人等咸
宜各安生業照常居住凡出售食物之人自必公平給價決不勒
措惟遇有執持槍械華人定必即行正法若由某房放槍即
將該房焚毀嗣後某國武官來索兵器有者即刻交出如有
隱匿一經覺查即將該房焚毀倘華人有搶奪情事亦立就地
正法各宜凜遵勿違特示

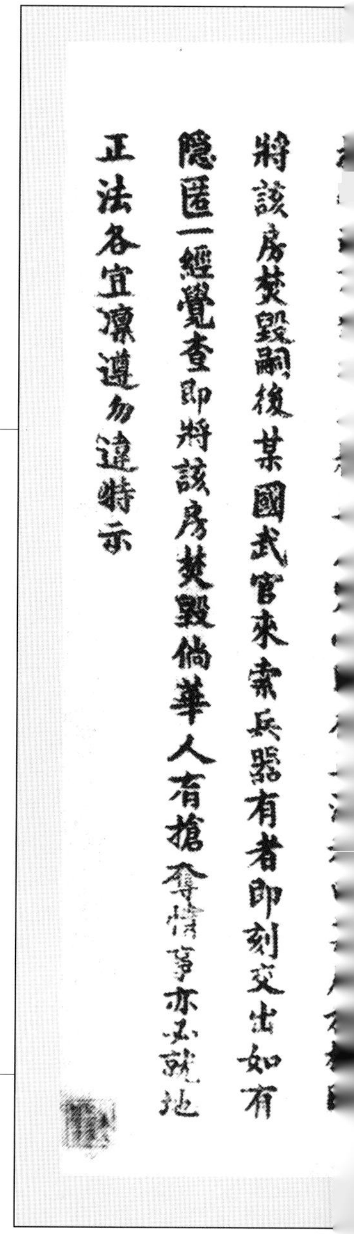
將該房焚毀嗣後某國武官來索兵器有者即刻交出如有
隱匿一經覺查即將該房焚毀倘華人有搶奪情事亦立就地
正法各宜凜遵勿違特示

联军对北京实行分区管理，镇压反抗。这是美军在自己管理的南城地区张贴的布告。

The Allied Forces put Beijing under control by divisions of areas to better suppress resistance. This is a notice posted by the Americans in the southern division under their control.

法军在自己所辖地区张贴布告。
A notice posted by French troops in the area under their control

▼ 俄军在自己所辖的东城地区张贴的布告。
A notice posted by Russian troops in the area under their control

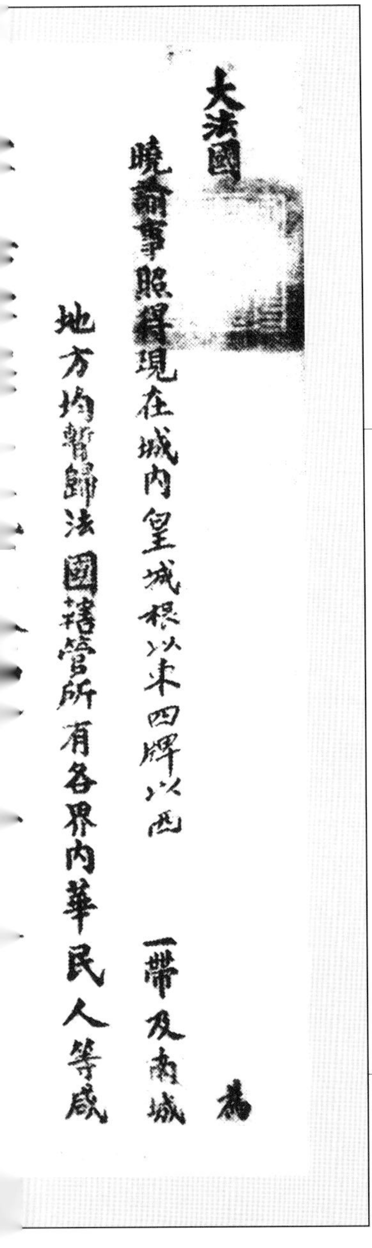

大法國　為
曉諭事照得現在城內皇城根以東四牌以西一帶及南城
地方均暫歸法國轄管所有各界內華民人等咸

大俄國　為
曉諭事照得現在城內北城根以南一帶及南城
地方均暫歸俄國轄管所有各界內華民人等咸
宜各安生業照常居住凡出售食物之人自必公平給價決不勒
措惟遇有執持槍械華人定必即行正法若由某房放槍即
將該房焚毀關役某國武官來索兵器有者[illegible]有
隱匿一經覺查即將該房焚毀倘華人有搶[illegible]
正法各宜凜遵勿違特示

俄军中的哥萨克士兵在京城驻地的营房前。
Cossack soldiers in the Russian troops in front of their barracks in Beijing

德军征用了一位清政府高级官员的大宅院，作为司令部。两位德军士兵穿着不合体的中式长皮袍站哨。
German troops appropriated the mansion of a high-ranking official of the Qing Government as their headquarters. The picture shows two German soldiers on duty wearing Chinese-style leather coats.

美军司令沙飞（左二）与前来议事的法军司令福里（左三）在先农坛的美军司令部合影。

US Commander Adna Romanza (*second left*) and French Commander Henri Nicolas Frey (*third left*) met at the headquarters of US troops in Xiannongtan.

法军在景山绮望楼安营扎寨。
French troops turned the lookout tower of the imperial garden of Jingshan into a barrack.

凡帝王专享的殿堂园苑，都驻进联军。这是皇宫内日军张灯结彩，迎度他们的天长节。
All halls and gardens exclusively used by the royal family were taken by foreign troops. The picture shows part of the imperial palace decorated by Japanese troops celebrating a Japanese festival.

高级军官们在紫禁城里留影。
High-ranking officers taking a photo in the Forbidden City

各国公使、商人纷纷进宫。这位先生在乾清宫的龙椅上，过了片刻皇帝瘾。

Foreign envoys and merchants streamed into the Imperial Palace. This man sits on the throne in the Qianqing Hall (Hall of Heavenly Purity).

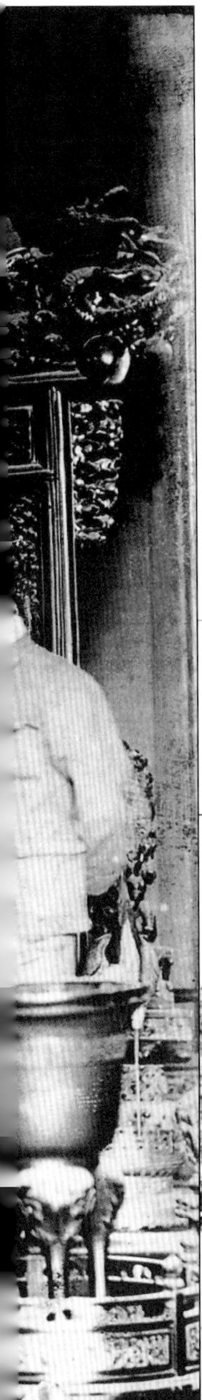

紫禁城在中国代表皇权的至高无上和尊严，联军为镇服中国人和羞辱清政府，举行穿越皇宫的阅兵游行。这是联军骑兵进入大清门。

The Forbidden City represented the supremacy and sanctity of imperial power in China. To conquer the Chinese people and humiliate the Qing Government, the Allied Forces held a parade in the palace. The picture shows the Allied Forces passing the gate of Daqingmen.

午门外的美军队列。
Formation of US troops outside the gate of Wumen

联军列队紫禁城神武门。
Allied Forces at the gate of Shenwumen

The War Before Neg

谈判前的战争与签约

ations and the Signing of the *Protocol of 1901*

就在联军占领北京的当天，远在德国的瓦德西元帅被列强各国任命为八国联军最高统帅。9月，瓦德西一到中国，就组织以德军为主的联军攻打山海关、保定、张家口和山西城镇，对清政府保持压力，迫使清政府做出更多的让步，以获取更大利益。

On the day the Allied Forces occupied Beijing, the powers appointed Field Marshal Waldersee, who was in Germany, supreme commander of the Eight-Power Allied Forces. As soon as Waldersee arrived in China in September, he led the Allied Forces, mainly composed of German troops, to attack Shanhaiguan, Baoding, Zhangjiakou and towns in Shanxi Province. The actions were designed to put pressure on the Qing Government and force it to make further concessions so the powers could procure more benefits.

乘清政府应付联军进攻之际，俄国沙皇尼古拉二世征调18万军队，自任总司令，分6路攻进中国东北。从7月初到10月底，相继攻陷哈尔滨、吉林、沈阳、锦州等大中城市，东三省到处可见俄军的身影。

While the Qing Government was struggling to stop the attack by the Allied Forces, Tsar Nicholas II of Russia had personally assumed the post of commander-in-chief to lead a force of 180,000 to attack northeast China via six routes. From early July to late October, Russian troops captured big and medium-sized cities, including Harbin, Jilin, Shenyang and Jinzhou. Russian soldiers were seen everywhere in the three provinces in northeast China.

瓦德西（1832-1904），德国陆军元帅。1900年8月在德国被八国推举为联军统帅，9月底赶到中国赴任，上任即指挥联军四处讨伐，扩大战争，坦言〝欲使外交方面略添生气，必须进行规模较大的军事行动。〞迫清政府在谈判桌上割让更多利益。

German Field Marshall Alfred Graf von Waldersee (1832-1904) was elected commander-in-chief of the Allied Forces in August 1900 while he was in Germany. In late September he came to China to take up the office. Shortly afterward he directed the Allied Forces to attack the Qing government forces, expanding the war. He said frankly, "To make diplomatic maneuvers to work, large-scale military actions must be taken" in order to pressure the Qing Government to make more concessions on the negotiating table.

9月30日，山海关守军在清政府"不许开衅"的命令下，将这个处于东北、华北之间的兵家必争之地，交给联军。一队英军已开至城下。

On September 30, under the order of "no provocation" by the Qing Government, Chinese troops stationed in Shanhaiguan Pass handed over the strategic military point between northeast China and north China to the Allied Forces. A British force arrived at the foot of the city wall.

山海关建于1381年，是明长城的最东端。清政府沿关设置了五座炮台。联军夺关后，炮台被均分给各国军队。这是俄国士兵占守的山海关东关。

Shanhaiguan Pass was built in 1381 as the easternmost end of the Ming Great Wall. The Qing Government had constructed five batteries along the pass. After the Allied Forces took the pass, the batteries fell into the hands of foreign troops. This is the eastern part of the pass occupied by Russian troops.

牧马山海关下的英军士兵。

A British soldier herding a horse at the foot of Shanhaiguan Pass

英军在关下的游动哨，发现了一户住在山洞里的居民。
British patrolling soldiers discover a family living in a cave at the foot of Shanhaiguan Pass.

10月，联军攻占秦皇岛，并在此建立联军过冬基地。图为联军控制下的秦皇岛灯塔区。

In October, the Allied Forces captured Qinhuangdao and built their winter base there. This is the Qinhuangdao lighthouse area under control of the Allied Forces.

德国人伦琴1895年发现了X光。5年后利用X光原理诊断战伤的仪器已出现在联军的野战医院。

In 1895, German scientist Wilhelm Conrad Roentgen discovered the X-ray. Five years later, medical instruments based on the X-ray theory appeared in field hospitals of the Allied Forces.

10月中旬，德、法、英、意集联军万余众，南下进攻直隶省城保定。这是奉命自天津向保定开进的英军。前行者为坎贝尔准将。

In mid-October, more than 10,000 German, French, British and Italian troops were moving southward to attack Baoding, then capital city of Zhili Province. In the front was Brigadier Campbell of the British troops marching from Tianjin to Baoding.

正与各国洽降的李鸿章，闻讯向镇守保定的代理直隶总督廷雍发电："勿轻用武挑衅，致启不测之祸。"未料，当廷雍率官员礼迎联军进城时，却遭逮捕。

Li Hongzhang, who was negotiating with the Allied Forces on surrender of the Qing troops, sent a telegram to Ting Yong, Acting Governor-General of Zhili Province, who was guarding Baoding, warning him "not to resort to military provocation rashly, or unexpected disaster will be triggered off." Ironically, Ting was arrested when he led officials to welcome the Allied Forces into the city.

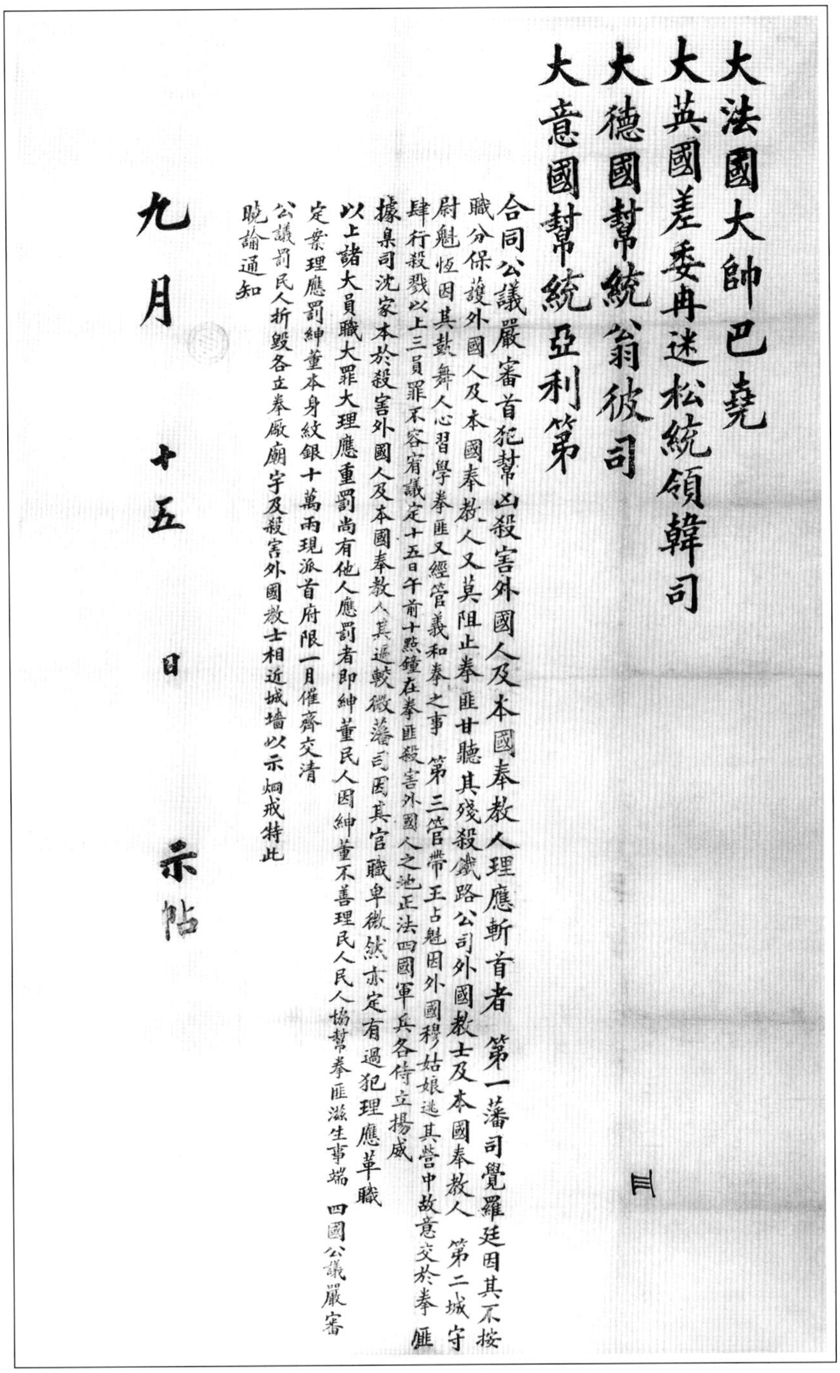

大法國大帥巴堯
大英國差委冉迷松統領韓司
大德國幫統翁彼司
大意國幫統亞利第
合同公議嚴審首犯幫凶殺害外國人及本國奉教人理應斬首者 第一藩司覺羅廷因其不按
職分保護外國人及本國奉教人又莫阻止拳匪甘聽其殘殺鐵路公司外國教士及本國奉教人 第二城守
尉魁恆因其鼓舞人心習學拳匪又經管義和拳之事 第三管帶王占魁因外國穆姑娘逃其營中故意交於拳匪
肆行殺戮以上三員罪不容宥議定十五日午前十點鐘在拳匪殺害外國人之地正法四國軍兵各侍立揚威
據臬司沈家本於殺害外國人及本國奉教人其遲較微藩司因其官職卑微然亦定有過犯理應革職
以上諸大員職大罪大理應重罰尚有他人應罰者即紳董民人因紳董不善理民人民人協幫拳匪滋生事端 四國公議嚴審
定案理應罰紳董本身紋銀十萬兩現派首府限一月催齊交清
公議罰民人折毀各立拳廠廟宇及殺害外國教士相近城墻以示炯戒特此
曉諭通知
九月 十五 日 示帖

11月初，身居清政府二品大员的廷雍和保定另两位官员被联军斩首示众。从联军这份光绪二十六年九月十五日（这一年旧历闰八月）的布告中可知，罪名是〝未按职分保护外国人〞等。对此，清政府反应：〝即使中国官员有办理不善之处，应交中国自行处分，何得侵我自主之权？〞

In early November, Ting Yong, a second-ranking official, and two other local officials of Baoding were beheaded and the bodies exhibited publicly. In this notice posted by Allied Forces on the 15th day of the 9th month of the 26th year of the Guangxu Reign, it stated they were given the death penalty for "not fulfilling their duty to protect foreigners." To this the Qing Government responded, "Even if Chinese officials had not properly handled the matter, they should be punished by the Chinese Government, how can our sovereignty be thus infringed upon?"

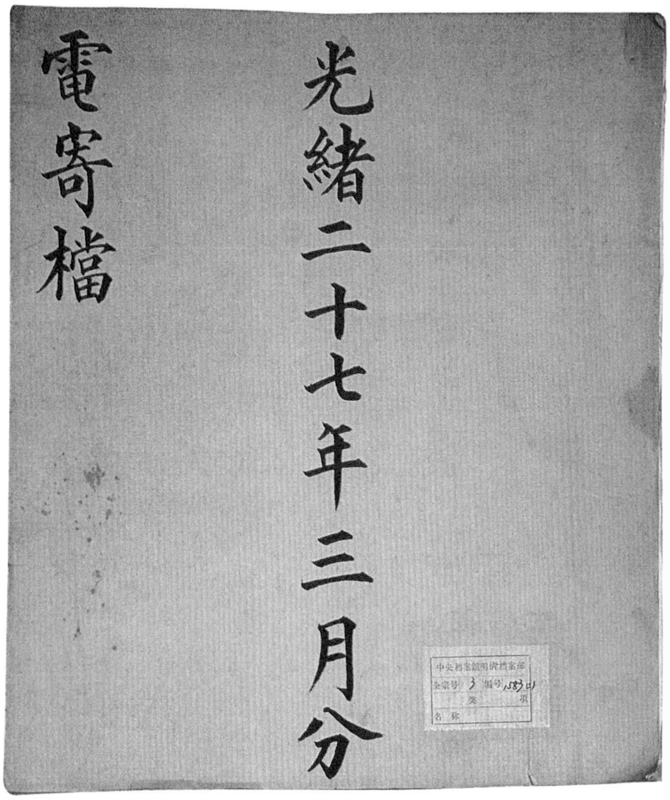
光緒二十七年三月分
電寄檔

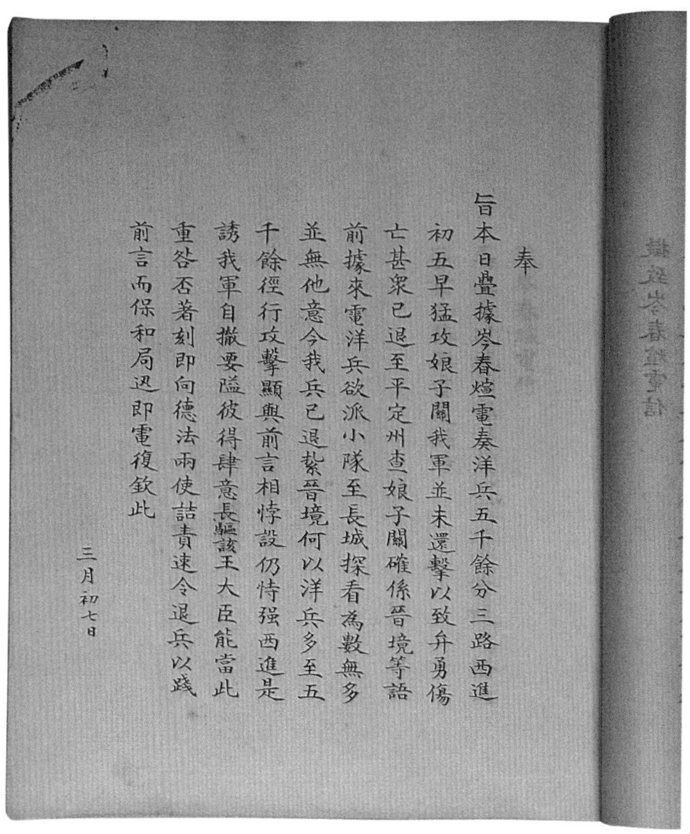
奉
旨本日疊據岑春煊電奏洋兵五千餘分三路西進初五早猛攻娘子關我軍並未還擊以致弁勇傷亡甚衆已退至平定州查娘子關確係晉境等語前據來電洋兵欲派小隊至長城探看為數無多並無他意今我兵已退紮晉境何以洋兵多至五千餘徑行攻擊顯與前言相悖設仍恃强西進是誘我軍自撤要隘彼得肆意長驅該王大臣能當此重咎否著刻即向德法兩使詰責速令退兵以踐前言而保和局迅即電復欽此

三月初七日

11月下旬，联军发兵山西。清政府责令正在北京与联军谈判的奕劻和李鸿章进行交涉。
In late November, the Allied Forces began to attack Shanxi. The Qing Government instructed Yi Kuang and Li Hongzhang, who were negotiating with the Allied Forces in Beijing, to handle the matter.

德军充当了进攻山西的主力。
German troops were the main force attacking Shanxi.

联军所到之处都有这样大规模屠杀中国百姓的场景。
Wherever the Allied Forces went, large-scale massacre took place.

瓦德西到京后，司令部设在"三海"中的仪鸾殿，这是他（中间站立者）与联军军官们在殿前合影。

When Waldersee came to Beijing, he set up his headquarters at the Yiluan Hall. The picture shows Waldersee (*middle*) and the officers of the Allied Forces in front of the hall.

1900年12月，联军成立"管理北京委员会"，代行政府司法、征税、维持秩序等职能。图为驻守东便门的俄军。

In December 1900, the Allied Forces set up the "Committee for the Management of Beijing" that performed judicial, taxation and public security functions. The picture shows Russian troops stationed at Dongbianmen.

法军在北京城乡间的要路设卡盘察、征税。

French troops set up stations for inspection and taxation on main roads linking the City of Beijing with the countryside.

城里，联军及其雇佣的华人刽子手仍在刑场忙碌。
Inside the city, the Allied Forces and their hired local men were busy executing people.

乡间，义和团团民被草率地就地正法的事不断发生。

In the countryside, many Boxers were executed on the spot.

纯属私家性质的、由北京大商号聚资组成的消防队——水会，被"管理北京委员会"无偿征用。

The Committee for the Management of Beijing appropriated the Water Society—a private fire brigade financed by major businesses in Beijing.

李鸿章（1823 - 1901）大学士，直隶总督兼北洋通商事务大臣。十九世纪六十年代，开办了一批军工厂和民用工厂并建立北洋水师。1875年以后，列强与中国所签的不平等条约，如《烟台条约》、《中法新约》、《马关条约》、《中俄密约》等尽系李鸿章代表谈判、签字。1900年10月被清政府任命为全权议和大臣，偕皇族奕劻亲王与各国公使谈判议和。

Li Hongzhang (1823-1901), Grand Secretary, Zhili Governor-General and Minister in Charge of Northern Trade Affairs. During the 1860s, a number of military and civilian factories and the Northern Navy were established on his orders. After 1875, Li was the chief negotiator representing the Qing Government and signed all unequal treaties forced upon China by the powers, including the *Agreement of Chefoo*, the Sino-French *Treaty of Tientsin*, the *Treaty of Shimonoseki* and the Sino-Russian *Contract for the Construction and Work of the Chinese Eastern Railway*. In October 1900, he was appointed by the Qing Government as minister plenipotentiary for peace negotiations and, together with Prince Yi Kuang, participated in peace negotiations with envoys of foreign nations.

图为11国公使——组成联军的八国加上西、比、荷三国，在共同商讨对中国的议和大纲。从1900年10月到是年年底，11国围绕谈判内容，争执不休，直到12月24日才统一了意见，向清政府提出了有12条条款的"议和大纲"。清政府被迫一条不改地接受列强的"议和大纲"为既定条约。这个大纲里，"道歉"、"惩凶"、"驻军"、"赔款"……但凡一个国家所珍惜的主权被践踏殆尽。这个议和大纲是《辛丑条约》的蓝本。

In this picture, envoys of 11 nations—the eight nations that formed the Eight-Power Allied Forces plus Spain, Belgium and Holland—are discussing the outline for peace negotiations with China. From October 1900, the 11 countries carried out a hot debate on the content of the negotiations before they reached a consensus on December 24. They proposed a 12-article "outline of peace negotiations" to the Qing Government, which was later forced to accept it without making any amendment. This outline, including such terms as "offering apology," "punishing murderers," "stationing armed forces," and "paying indemnities," trampled on all sovereignties cherished by any nation. This outline was the blueprint of the *Protocol of 1901*.

联军统帅瓦德西，配合谈判，在午门前进行又一次示威性阅兵。

Commander-in-Chief Waldersee held a parade in front of the gate of Wumen to demonstrate support to the Allied Forces in their negotiations with the Qing Government.

《辛丑条约》签订仪式。左为十一国公使，右为清政府代表奕劻（前）、李鸿章（后）。时间：1901 年 9 月 7 日。这一年，中国旧历为辛丑年。

The signing ceremony of the *Protocol of 1901*. On the left were envoys of the 11 nations while on the right were representatives of the Qing Government, Yi Kuang (*front*) and Li Hongzhang (*rear*). The event took place on September 7, 1901, the Year of Xinchou in Chinese lunar calendar.

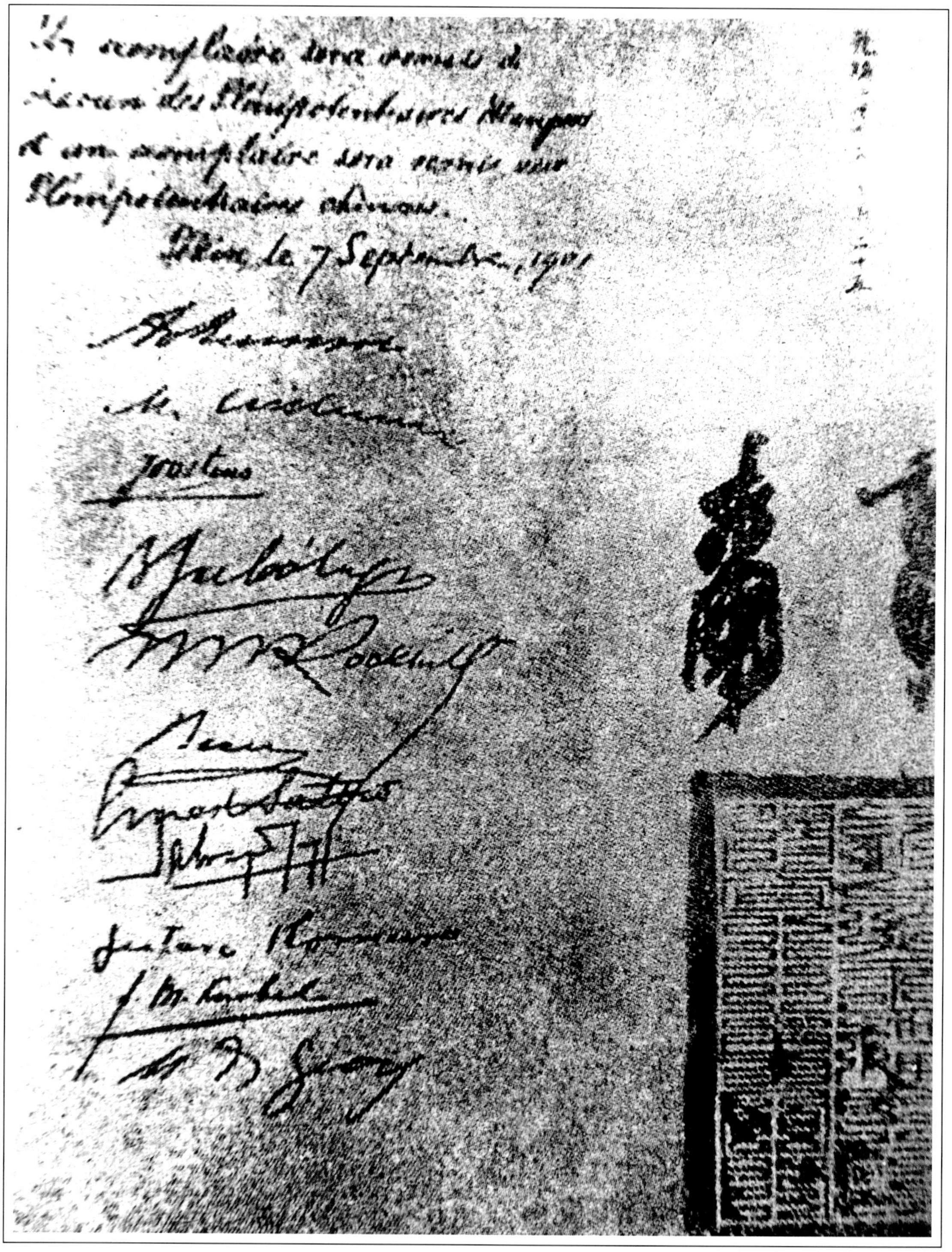

Un exemplaire sera remis à chacun des Plénipotentiaires étrangers et un exemplaire sera remis au Plénipotentiaire chinois.

Pékin, le 7 Septembre 1901

《辛丑条约》文本局部。

Part of the text of the *Protocol of 1901*.

《辛丑条约》内容提要

第一、第三款，均为道歉，即指定亲王载沣率团赴德国为克林德之死谢罪，指定户部侍郎那桐率团赴日本为杉山彬之死谢罪。第二款，规定清政府"惩凶"，并开列了名单，按名处罚利用义和团及开罪了外国人的大臣以及各省地方官员。那些在义和团运动期间有过排外行为的地方，一律停止五年科举考试。第四款，对于在义和团运动期间被毁的传教士坟墓，由清政府出资，使馆派人监督，确保修复好。第五款，两年以内，中国不准进口军火。第六款，中国按海关银价赔款4亿5千万两，年息4厘，每6个月付给1次，总计9亿8千万两，分39年付清。第七款，列强派遣军队保护北京使馆。第八款，大沽炮台及北京与大沽间的所有炮台，一律拆除。第九款，列强在京津、津榆铁路沿线城市驻军。第十款，永远禁止中国人参加带有排外性质的任何组织，以及各省督、抚以下的地方官员们，对其辖区内出现的任何排外行为，如不即行镇压，立刻革职。第十一款，清政府出资改善并维护内河河道，以便利各国到中国内地通商。第十二款，清政府改总理各国事务衙门为外务部，班列六部之前。

Abstract of the *Protocol of 1901*

Articles 1 and 3: Prince Zai Feng shall head a delegation to Germany to offer an apology for the death of Ketteler, and Minister of Revenue Na Tong shall head a delegation to Japan to offer an apology for the death of Aki Sugiyama. Article 2: The Qing Government shall, according to the given name list, punish the ministers and local officials who have made use of the Boxer Uprising to offend foreigners. The imperial examination shall be suspended for five years in regions that engaged in anti-foreign activities during the Boxer Uprising. Article 4: The Qing Government shall fund the repair of the graves of missionaries, which were destroyed during the Boxer Uprising, under the supervision of representatives sent by the legations. Article 5: China shall not import any arms for two years. Article 6: China shall pay 450 million taels of silver in indemnity according to Customs price, with an annual interest of 4 percent. The total amount of 980 million taels of silver shall be paid off in 39 years, with one payment per six months. Article 7: Foreign countries shall dispatch armed forces to protect their legations in Beijing. Article 8: Dagu Fort and all other forts between Beijing and Dagu shall be demolished. Article 9: The foreign powers shall station armed forces in cities along the Beijing-Tianjin Railway. Article 10: Chinese shall never be allowed to join any anti-foreign organization. Local officials under the level of provincial governor and prefecture magistrate, who failed to immediately suppress anti-foreign activities in areas under their jurisdiction, shall be removed from office. Article 11: The Qing Government shall appropriate funds for improving and maintaining inland river courses for the convenience of the nations to do business in inland areas of China. Article 12: The Qing Government shall change the Office for the Management of Business of All Foreign Countries to the Ministry of Foreign Affairs, and place it on top of the six ministries.

清政府中央机要部门北档房代行尚书职权的左侍郎唐文治（1865 – 1954）亲手录记了《辛丑条约》条款全文（见卷首）。唐文治曾在清政府户部、总理各国事务衙门、外务部等任职。此手记现存于中国第一历史档案馆。

The full text of the *Protocol of 1901* (See the beginning of the book) was written down by Tang Wenzhi (1865-1954), Vice Minister and Acting Minister of North Archives, the central department in charge of confidential work in the Qing Government. Tang had worked with the Ministry of Revenue, the Office for Management of Business of All Foreign Countries and the Ministry of Foreign Affairs. The scripts are now in the collection of the First Historical Archives of China.

辛丑条约下的中国

China Under the *Protocol of 1901*

1901年是中国旧历辛丑年，在这一年，中国被迫接受了列强各国拟好的谈判条件。9月7日，正式签订了条约，史称《辛丑条约》。这一条约，使中国的主权、人权受尽侵凌。

In 1901, China was forced to accept the terms drawn up by the foreign powers for negotiations. On September 7, a treaty was formally signed, which is historically known as the *Protocol of 1901*. This treaty tramped on China's sovereignty and human rights to the utmost.

条约：永远禁止中国人参加带有排外性质的任何组织，违者处死。

The Protocol: Chinese people shall never be allowed to set up or join organizations that are hostile to other nations. Any violators shall be beheaded.

条约签订。列强承认慈禧太后执政合法，同意“两宫仍旧临朝”。慈禧挟光绪皇帝自西安启程，1902年1月3日回到北京。

With the signing of the treaty, the foreign powers recognized the legitimacy of the rule of Empress Dowager Cixi who, holding Emperor Guangxu under duress, left Xi'an and returned to Beijing on January 3, 1902.

清政府对义和团、对不甘亡国的仁人志士残酷镇压。这些上着重镣的，怀疑是义和团的男男女女，被迫为狱方劳动，他们随时可能被送上刑场。

The Qing Government did its utmost to suppress the Boxers and all those who were unwilling to see their country conquered by the Western powers. The men and women in the picture were suspected to be Boxers. Shackled, they were forced to work in prison and might be executed at any time.

北京的街头刑场，又一个受刑者，被刽子手按倒在地。
An execution ground in a street of Beijing. Another Chinese was to be executed.

人头成堆。
Heads cut off

对组织会党，旨在驱逐列强，推翻满清政府的革命党人，清政府视为“大逆”，施以凌迟酷刑处死。这组照片反映了被害人被肢解的全过程。

凌迟一。

People organized societies and parties to drive the foreign powers out of China and to overthrow the Qing Government. Regarding members of such revolutionary parties as committing "the monstrous crime of insubordination," the Qing Government put them to death by dismembering the body. Pictures here display the whole process of dismemberment.

Dismembering the body (I).

凌迟二。

Dismembering the body (II)

凌迟三

Dismembering the body (III)

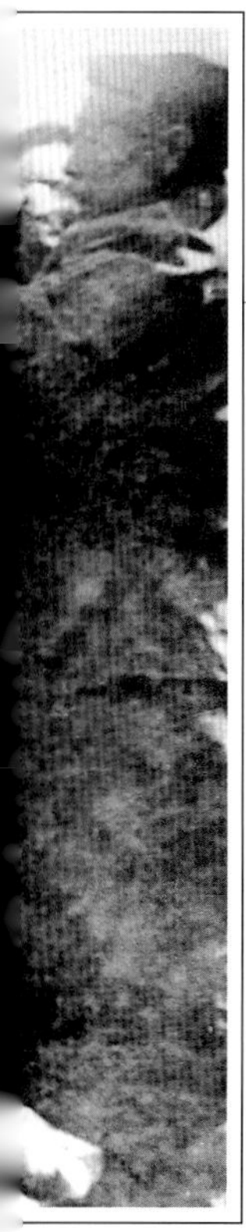

凌迟四

Dismembering the body (IV)

条约：惩办祸首

The Protocol: Punish chief offenders.

山西巡抚毓贤，任职期间曾下令处死了一批教士、教民，被列强定为必欲处决的官员之一。《辛丑条约》签订前，他已被撤职，流放新疆。签约后，清政府追发一道圣旨，将行至兰州的毓贤斩首。（见 196 页上谕）

Yu Xian, Governor of Shanxi Province, had ordered the killing of a group of missionaries and Chinese converts during his tenure of office. The foreign powers listed him as one of the officials who must be put to death. Before the signing of the *Protocol of 1901*, he was removed from his office and exiled to Xinjiang. After the treaty was signed, the Qing Government issued another edict and put Yu to death in Lanzhou, Gansu Province. (See the imperial edict on p.196)

一位高官即将就刑。史书记载，这时期北京菜市口刑场斩首的清政府高官仅有礼部尚书启秀和刑部左侍郎徐承煜。
A high-ranking official about to be executed. Historical records show that Qi Xiu, Minister of Rites and Education, and Xu Chengyu, Vice Minister of Justice,were the only high-ranking officials of the Qing Government put to death at the Caishikou execution ground.

清政府官员为保住官位，纷纷与教会修好。
To save their positions, officials of the Qing Government rushed to establish friendly relations with the church.

关于支付赔款的上谕。

An imperial edict on the payment of indemnities

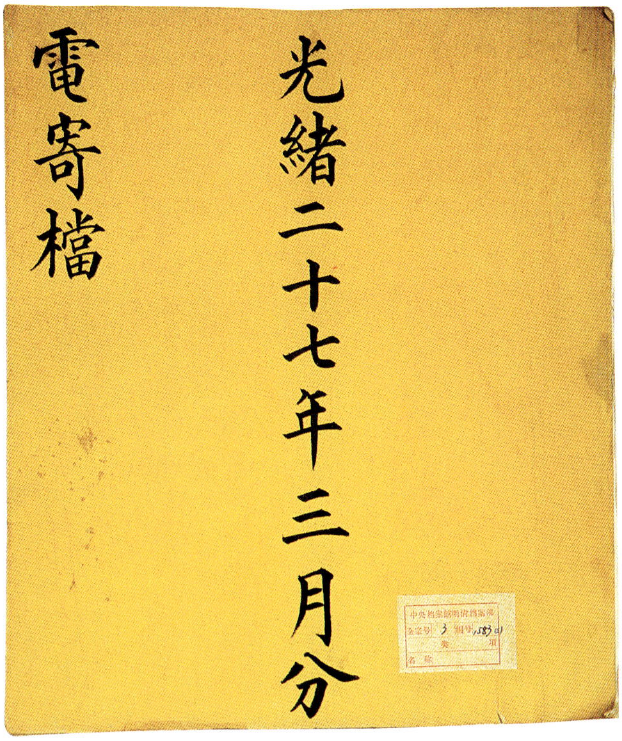
光緒二十七年三月分

電寄檔

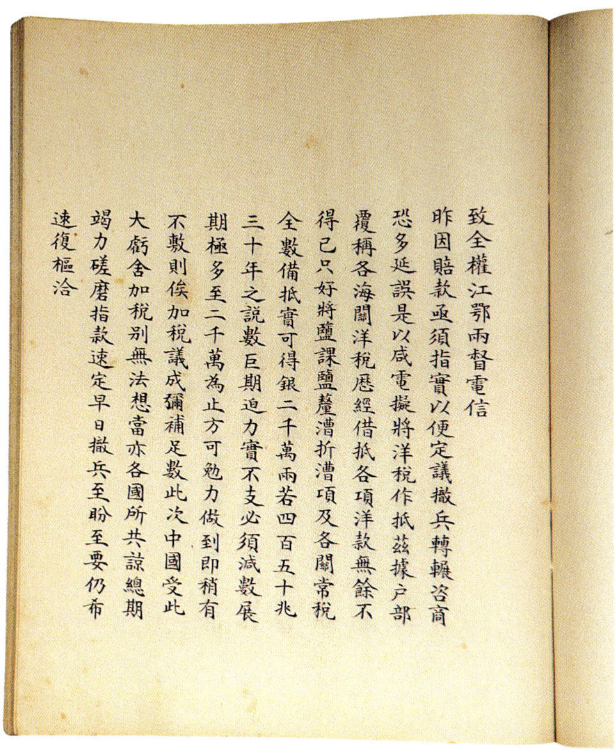
致全權江鄂兩督電信

昨因賠款亟須指實以便定議撤兵轉輾咨商恐多延誤是以咸電擬將洋稅作抵茲據户部覆稱各海關洋稅歷經借抵各項洋款無餘不得已只好將鹽課鹽釐漕折漕項及各關常稅全數備抵實可得銀二千萬兩若四百五十兆三十年之說數巨期迫力實不支必須減數展期極多至二千萬為止方可勉力做到即稍有不敷則俟加稅議成彌補足數此次中國受此大虧舍加稅别無法想當亦各國所共諒總期竭力磋磨指款速定早日撤兵至盼至要仍布速復樞洽

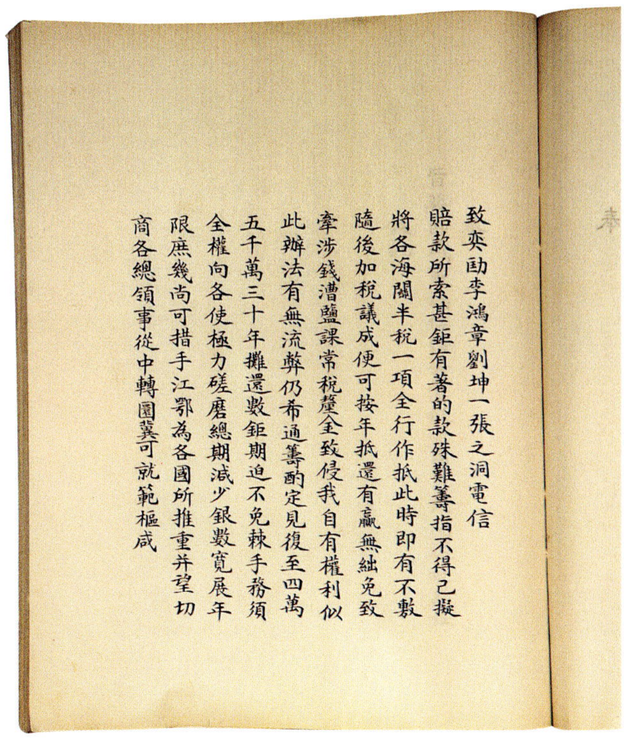
致奕劻李鴻章劉坤一張之洞電信

賠款所索甚鉅有著的款殊難籌指不得已擬將各海關半稅一項全行作抵此時即有不敷隨後加稅議成便可按年抵還有贏無絀免致牽涉錢漕鹽課常稅釐金致侵我自有權利似此辦法有無流弊仍希通籌酌定見復至四萬五千萬三十年攤還數鉅期迫不免棘手務須全權向各使極力磋磨總期減少銀數寬展年限庶幾尚可措手江鄂為各國所推重并望切商各總領事從中轉圜冀可就範樞咸

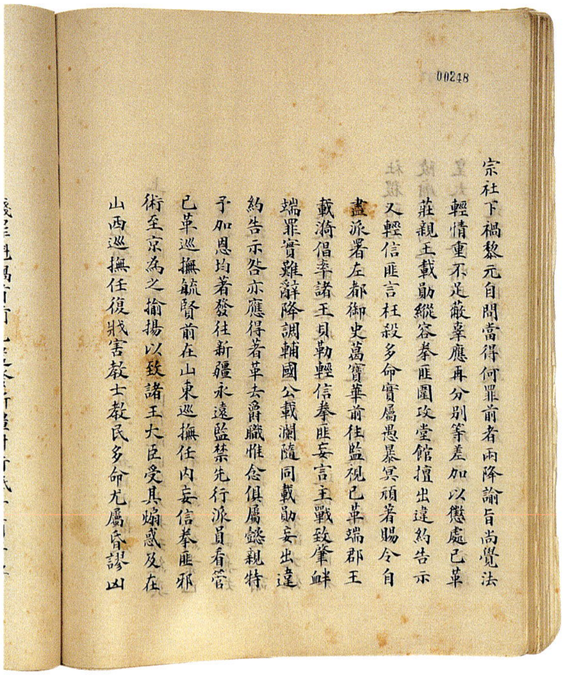

00248

宗社下禍黎元自問當得何罪前者兩降諭旨尚覺法
輕情重不足蔽辜應再分別等差加以懲處已革
莊親王載勛縱容拳匪圍攻堂館擅出違約告示
又輕信匪言枉殺多命實屬愚暴冥頑著賜令自
盡派署左都御史葛寶華前往監視已革端郡王
載漪倡率諸王貝勒輕信拳匪妄言主戰致肇衅
端罪實難辭降調輔國公載瀾隨同載勛妄出違
約告示咎亦應得著革去爵職惟念俱屬懿親特
予加恩均著發往新疆永遠監禁先行派員看管
已革巡撫毓賢前在山東巡撫任內妄信拳匪邪
術至京為之揄揚以致諸王大臣受其煽惑及在
山西巡撫任復戕害教士教民多命尤屬昏謬凶

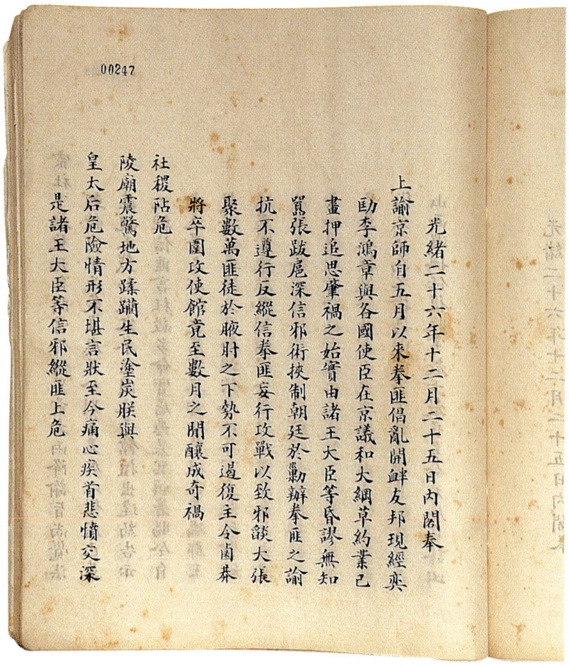

00247

光緒二十六年十二月二十五日內閣奉
上諭京師自五月以來拳匪倡亂開衅友邦現經奕
劻李鴻章與各國使臣在京議和大綱草約業已
畫押追思肇禍之始實由諸王大臣等昏謬無知
囂張跋扈深信邪術挾制朝廷於勦辦拳匪之諭
抗不遵行反縱信拳匪妄行攻戰以致邪燄大張
聚數萬匪徒於腋肘之下勢不可遏復主令鹵莽
將卒圍攻使館竟至數月之間釀成奇禍
社稷阽危
陵廟震驚地方蹂躪生民塗炭朕與
皇太后危險情形不堪言狀至今痛心疾首悲憤交深
是諸王大臣等信邪縱匪上危

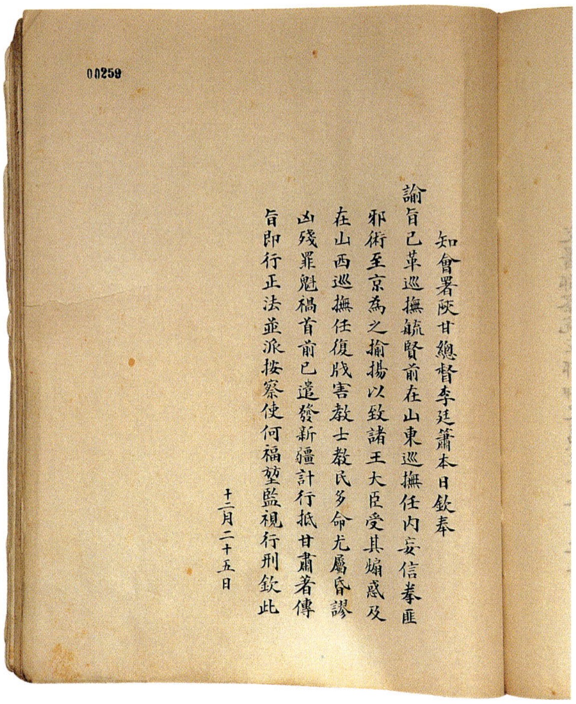

00259

知會署陝甘總督李廷簫本日欽奉
諭旨已革巡撫毓賢前在山東巡撫任內妄信拳匪
邪術至京為之揄揚以致諸王大臣受其煽惑及
在山西巡撫任復戕害教士教民多命尤屬昏謬
凶殘罪魁禍首前已遣發新疆計行抵甘肅著傳
旨即行正法並派按察使何福堃監視行刑欽此

十二月二十五日

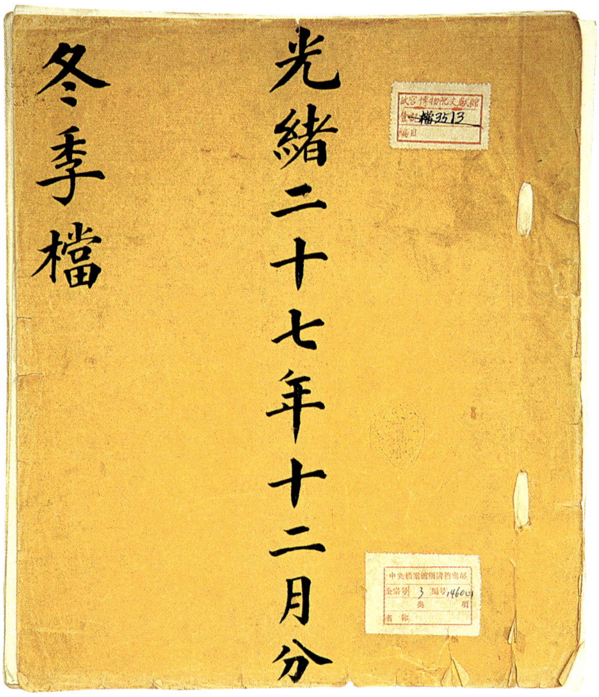

关于处死毓贤的上谕。

The imperial edict on the execution of Yu Xian

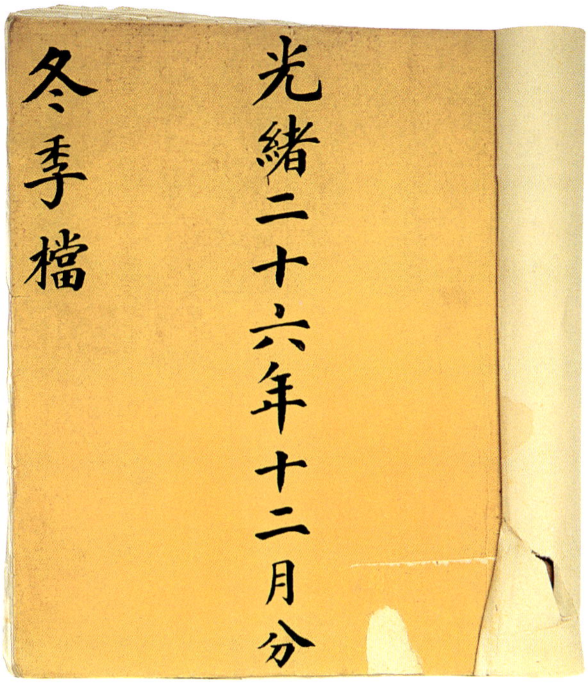

关于惩处官员的上谕。

An imperial edict on punishing officials

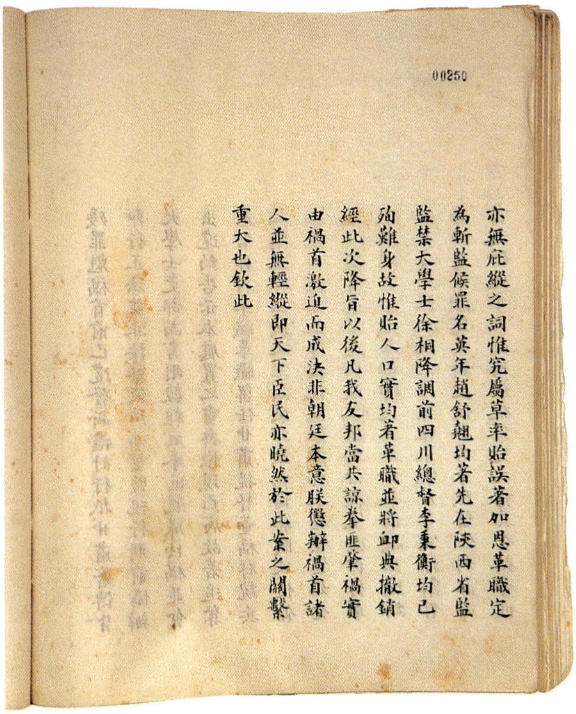

00250

亦無庇縱之詞惟究屬草率貽誤著加恩革職定
為斬監候罪名英年趙舒翹均著先在陝西省監
監禁大學士徐桐降調前四川總督李秉衡均已
殉難身故惟貽人口實均著革職並將卹典撤銷
經此次降旨以後凡我友邦當共諒拳匪肇禍實
由禍首激迫而成決非朝廷本意朕懲辦禍首諸
人並無輕縱即天下臣民亦曉然於此案之關繫
重大也欽此

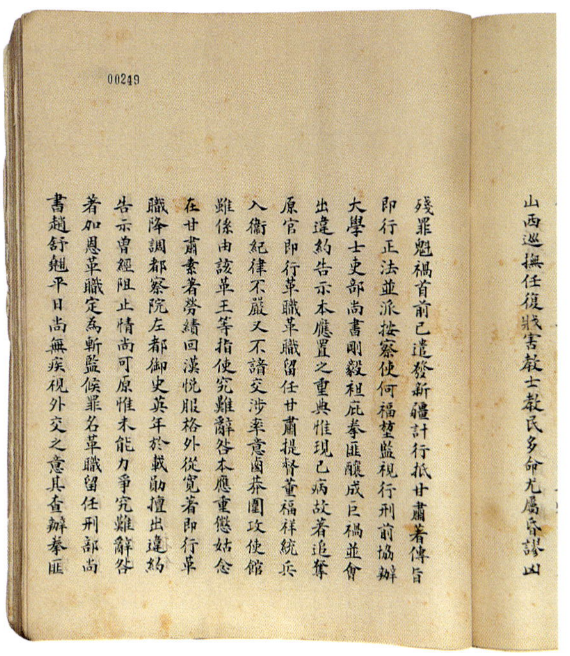

00249

山西巡撫任復戕害教士教民多命尤屬昏謬凶
殘罪魁禍首前已遣發新疆計行抵甘肅著傳旨
即行正法並派按察使何福堃監視行刑前協辦
大學士吏部尚書剛毅袒庇拳匪釀成巨禍並曾
出違約告示本應置之重典惟現已病故著追奪
原官即行革職革職留任甘肅提督董福祥統兵
入衛紀律不嚴又不諳交涉率意鹵莽圍攻使館
雖係由該革王等指使究難辭咎本應重懲姑念
在甘肅素著勞績回漢悅服格外從寬著即行革
職降調都察院左都御史英年於載勛擅出違約
告示曾經阻止情尚可原惟未能力爭究難辭咎
著加恩革職定為斬監候罪名革職留任刑部尚
書趙舒翹平日尚無疾視外交之意其查辦拳匪

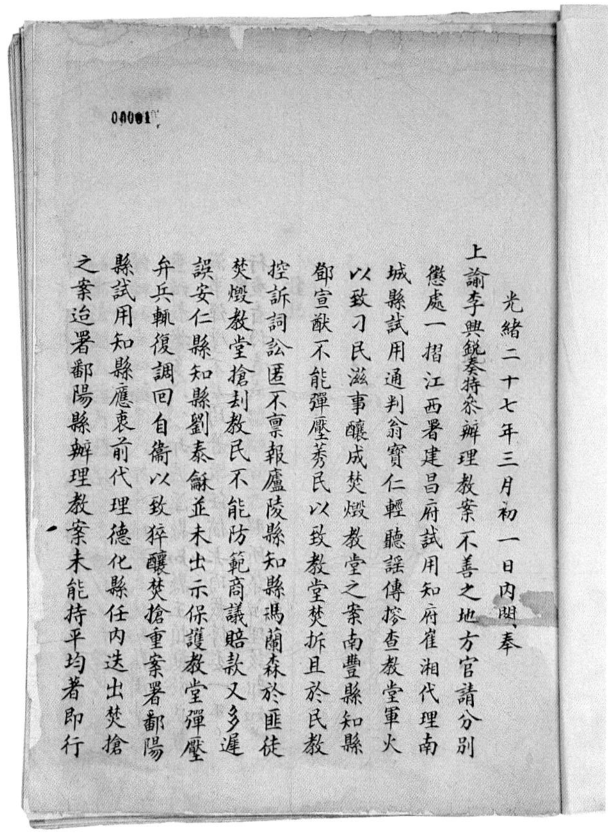

00001

光緒二十七年三月初一日内閣奉
上諭李興銳奏特參辦理教案不善之地方官請分別
懲處一摺江西署建昌府試用知府崔湘代理南
城縣試用通判翁寶仁輕聽謡傳掺查教堂軍火
以致刁民滋事釀成焚燬教堂之案南豐縣知縣
鄧宣猷不能彈壓莠民以致教堂焚拆且於民教
控訴詞訟匿不稟報廬陵縣知縣馮蘭森於匪徒
焚燬教堂搶刦教民不能防範商議賠款又多遲
誤安仁縣知縣劉泰龢並未出示保護教堂彈壓
弁兵輒復調回自衛以致猝釀焚搶重案署鄱陽
縣試用知縣應衷前代理德化縣任内迭出焚搶
之案迨署鄱陽縣辦理教案未能持平均著即行

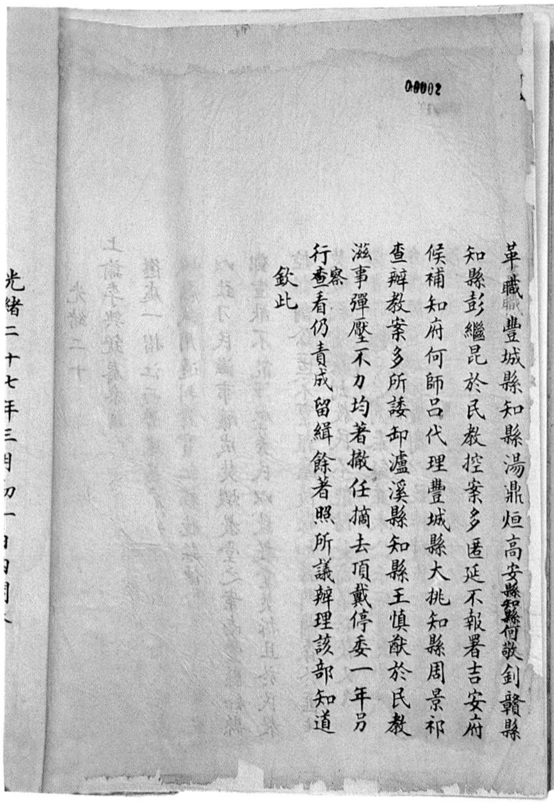

00002

革職豐城縣知縣湯鼎烜高安縣知縣何敬釗贛縣
知縣彭繼昆於民教控案多匿延不報署吉安府
候補知府何師呂代理豐城縣大挑知縣周景祁
查辦教案多所諉卸瀘溪縣知縣王慎猷於民教
滋事彈壓不力均著撤任摘去頂戴停委一年另
行查察看仍責成留緝餘著照所議辦理該部知道
欽此

光緒二十七年三月初一日内閣

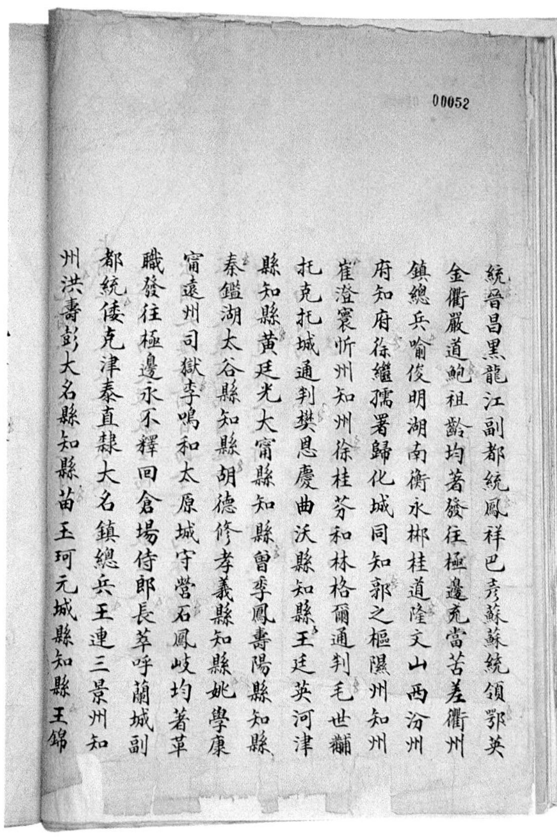

00052

統晉昌黑龍江副都統鳳祥巴彥蘇蘇統領鄂英
金衢嚴道鮑祖齡均著發往極邊充當苦差衢州
鎮總兵喻俊明湖南衡永郴桂道隆文山西汾州
府知府徐繼孺署歸化城同知郭之樞隰州知州
崔澄寰忻州知州徐桂芬和林格爾通判毛世黼
托克托城通判樊恩慶曲沃縣知縣王廷英河津
縣知縣黄廷光大甯縣知縣曾季鳳壽陽縣知縣
秦鑑湖太谷縣知縣胡德修孝義縣知縣姚學康
甯遠州司獄李鳴和太原城守營石鳳岐均著革
職發往極邊永不釋回倉場侍郎長萃呼蘭城副
都統倭克津泰直隸大名鎮總兵王連三景州知
州洪壽彭大名縣知縣苗玉珂元城縣知縣王錦

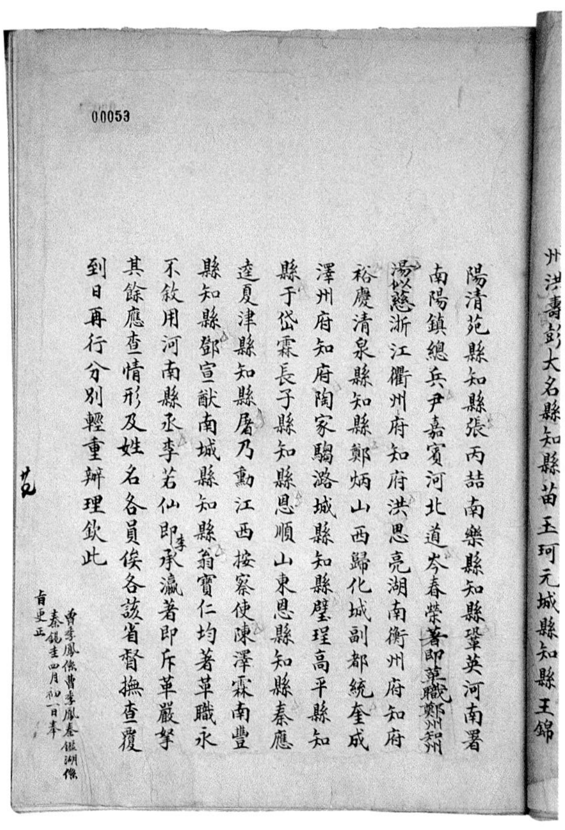

00053

州洪壽彭大名縣知縣苗玉珂元城縣知縣王錦
陽清苑縣知縣張丙喆南樂縣知縣翟英河南署
南陽鎮總兵尹嘉賓河北道岑春榮著即革職鄭州知州
湯似慈浙江衢州府知府洪思亮湖南衡州府知府
裕慶清泉縣知縣鄭炳山西歸化城副都統奎成
澤州府知府陶家騊潞城縣知縣璧理高平縣知
縣于岱霖長子縣知縣恩順山東恩縣知縣秦應
逵夏津縣知縣屠乃勳江西按察使陳澤霖南豐
縣知縣鄧宣猷南城縣知縣翁寶仁均著革職永
不敘用河南縣丞李若仙即李承瀛著即斥革嚴拏
其餘應查情形及姓名各員俟各該省督撫查覆
到日再行分別輕重辦理欽此

曾季鳳係曹季鳳秦鑑湖係
秦錫圭四月初一日奉
旨更正

关于惩处官员的上谕。
An imperial edict on punishing officials

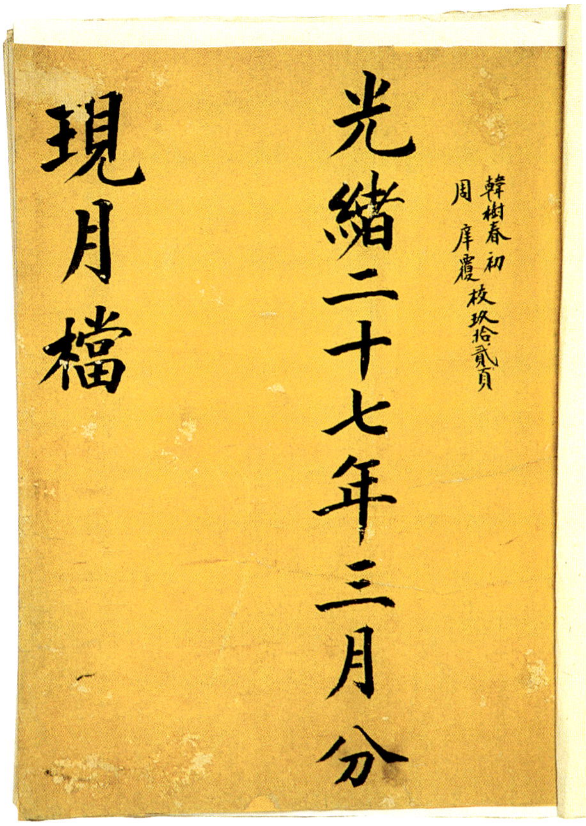

光緒二十七年三月分

韓樹春初 周庠霞校 玖拾貳頁

現月檔

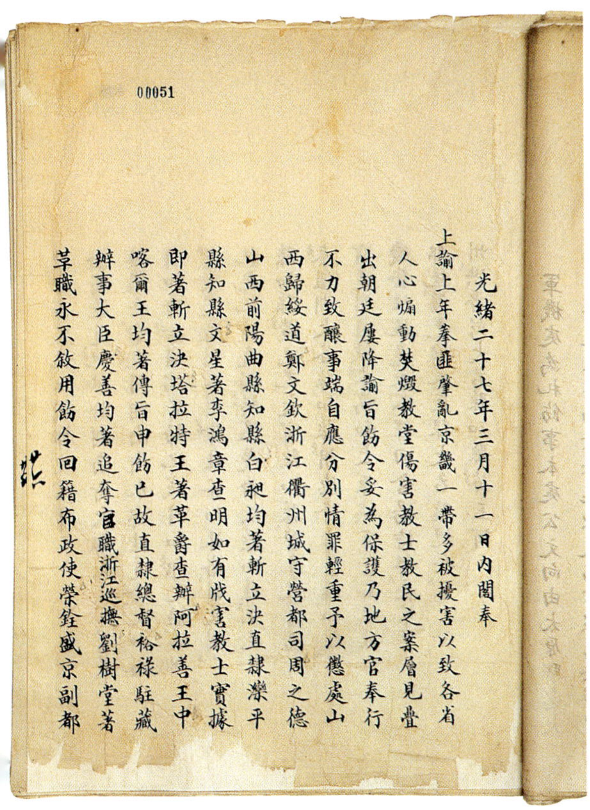

00051

光緒二十七年三月十一日內閣奉

上諭上年拳匪肇亂京畿一帶多被擾害以致各省人心煽動焚燬教堂傷害教士教民之案層見疊出朝廷屢降諭旨飭令妥為保護乃地方官奉行不力致釀事端自應分別情罪輕重予以懲處山西歸綏道鄭文欽浙江衢州城守營都司周之德山西前陽曲縣知縣白昶均著斬立決直隸欒平縣知縣文星著李鴻章查明如有戕害教士實據即著斬立決塔拉特王著革爵查辦阿拉善王中喀爾王均著傳旨申飭已故直隸總督裕祿駐藏辦事大臣慶善均著追奪官職浙江巡撫劉樹堂著革職永不敘用飭令回籍布政使榮銓盛京副都

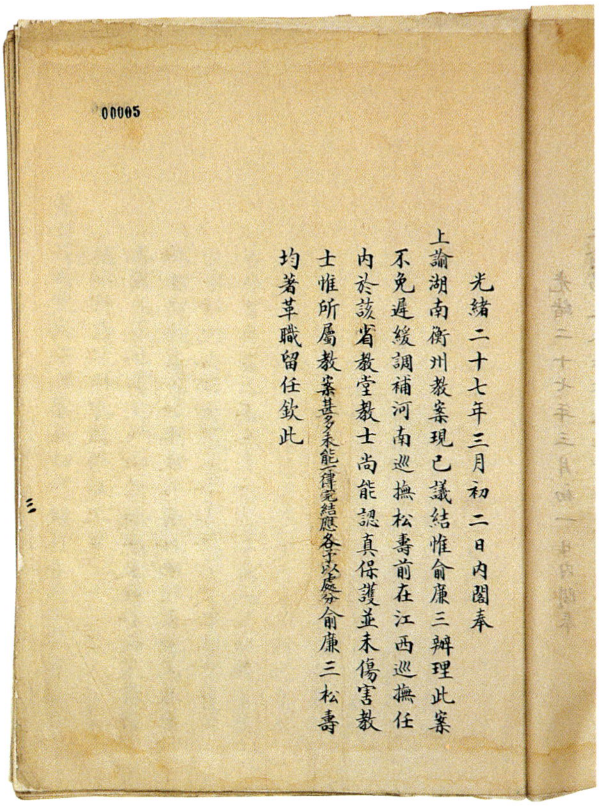

00005

光緒二十七年三月初二日內閣奉

上諭湖南衡州教案現已議結惟俞廉三辦理此案不免遲緩調補河南巡撫松壽前在江西巡撫任內於該省教堂教士尚能認真保護並未傷害教士惟所屬教案甚多未能一律完結應各予以處分俞廉三松壽均著革職留任欽此

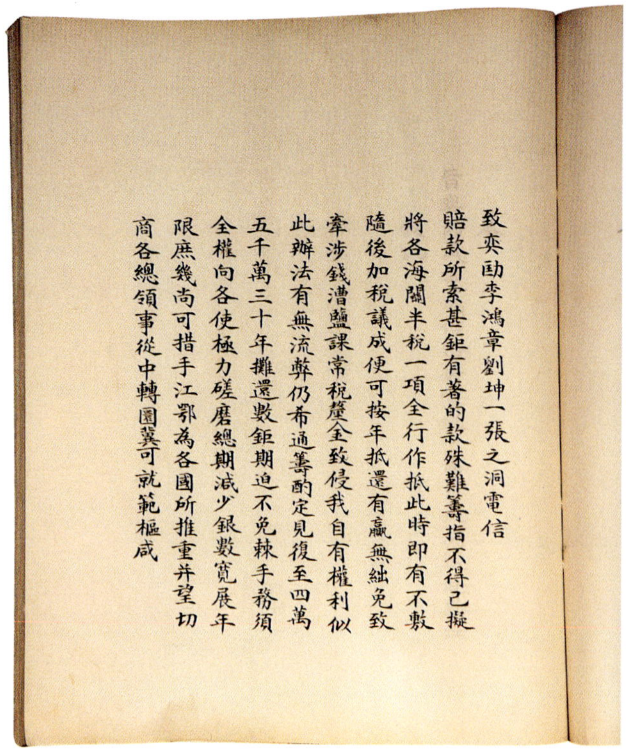

致奕劻李鴻章劉坤一張之洞電信

賠款所索甚鉅有著的款殊難籌指不得已擬將各海關半税一項全行作抵此時即有不敷隨後加税議成便可按年抵還有贏無絀免致牽涉錢漕鹽課常税釐金致侵我自有權利似此辦法有無流弊仍希通籌酌定見復至四萬五千萬三十年攤還數鉅期迫不免棘手務須全權向各使極力磋磨總期減少銀數寬展年限庶幾尚可措手江鄂為各國所推重并望切商各總領事從中轉圜冀可就範樞咸

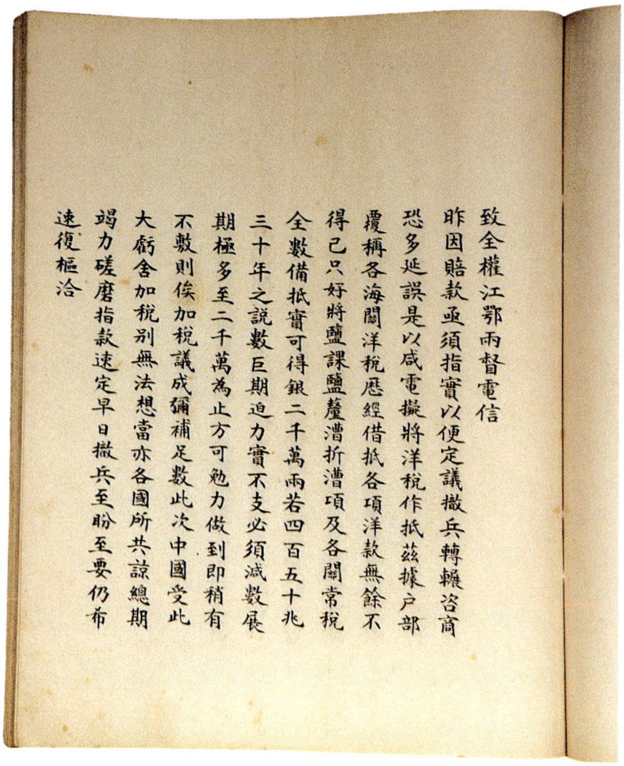

致全權江鄂兩督電信

昨因賠款亟須指實以便定議撤兵轉輾咨商恐多延誤是以咸電擬將洋税作抵茲據户部覆稱各海關洋税歷經借抵各項洋款無餘不得已只好將鹽課鹽釐漕折漕項及各關常税全數備抵實可得銀二千萬兩若四百五十兆三十年之説數巨期迫力實不支必須減數展期極多至二千萬為止方可勉力做到即稍有不敷則俟加税議成彌補足數此次中國受此大虧舍加税别無法想當亦各國所共諒總期竭力磋磨指款速定早日撤兵至盼至要仍希速復樞洽

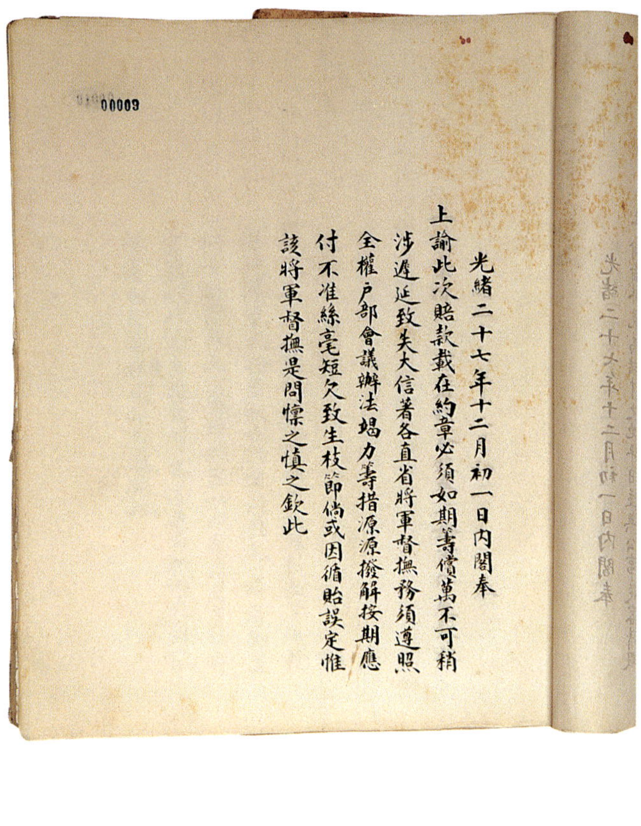

光緒二十七年十二月初一日内閣奉

上諭此次賠款載在約章必須如期籌償萬不可稍涉遲延致失大信著各直省將軍督撫務須遵照全權户部會議辦法竭力籌措源源撥解按期應付不准絲毫短欠致生枝節倘或因循貽誤定惟該將軍督撫是問懍之慎之欽此

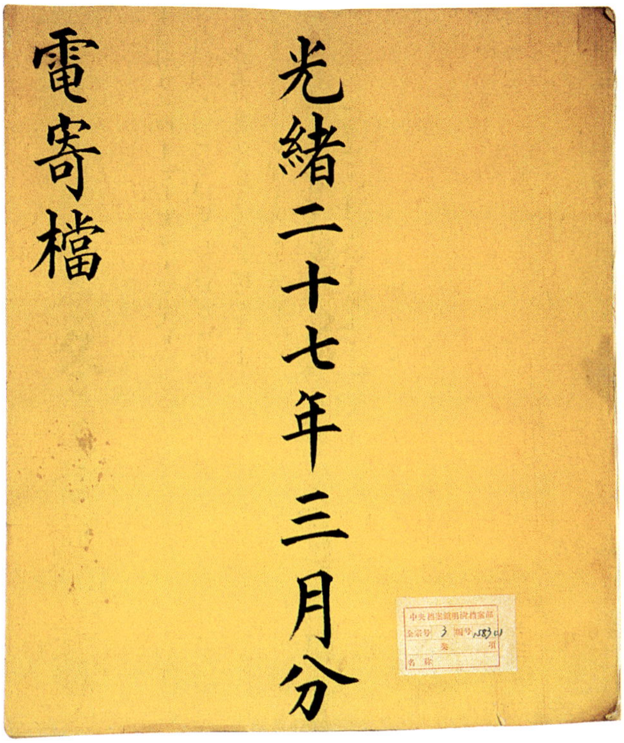

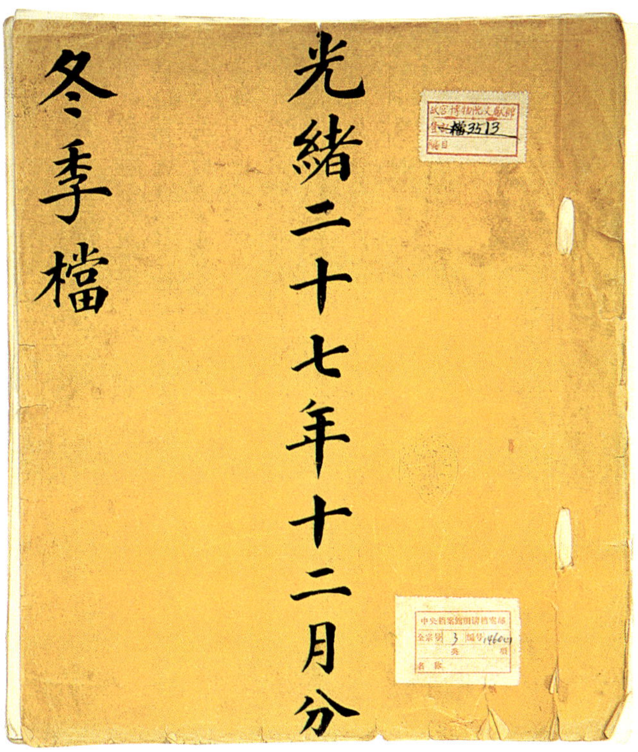

关于筹付赔银的上谕。
An imperial edict on raising funds to pay the indemnities

条约: 有过排外行为的地方，一律停止五年科举考试。

The Protocol: The imperial examination shall be suspended for five years in regions that engaged in anti-foreign activities.

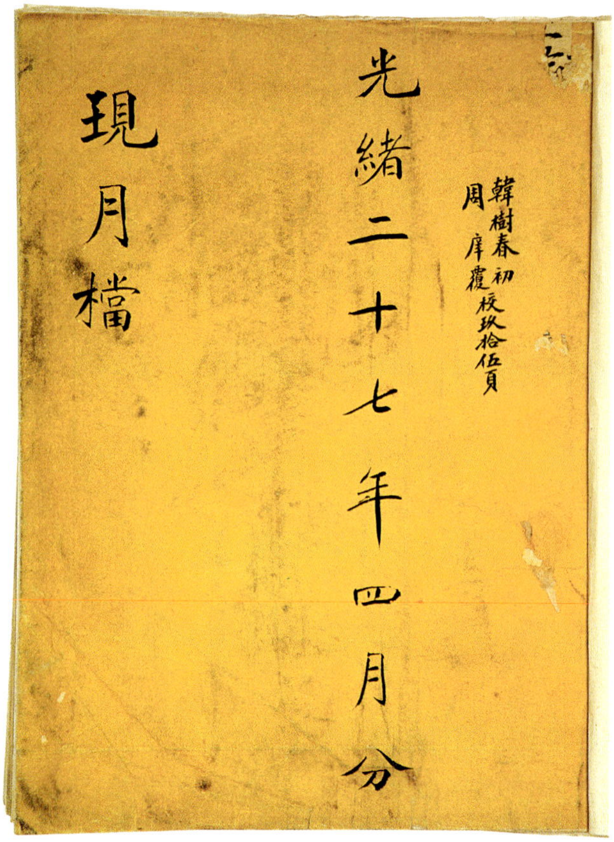

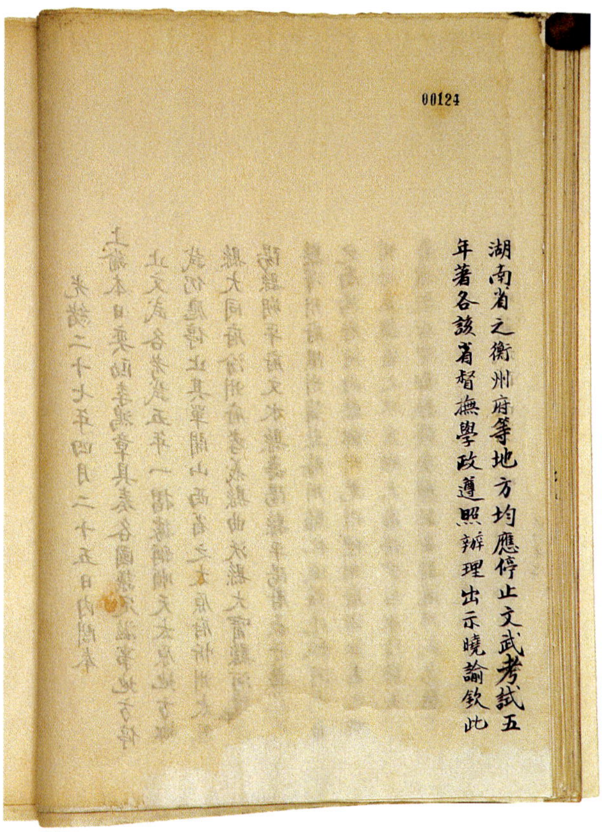
00124

湖南省之衡州府等地方均應停止文武考試五
年著各該省督撫學政遵照辦理出示曉諭欽此

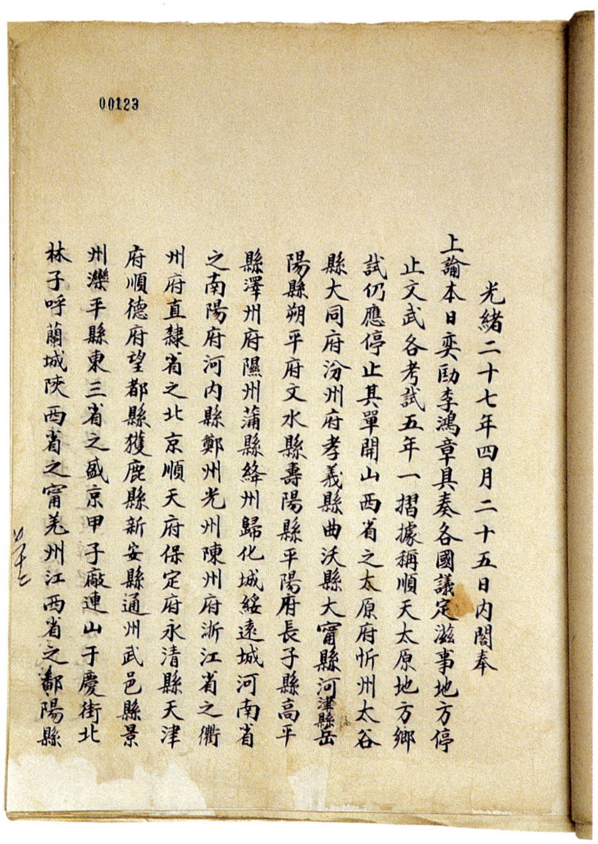
00123

光緒二十七年四月二十五日內閣奉
上諭本日奕劻李鴻章具奏各國議定滋事地方停
止文武各考試五年一摺據稱順天太原地方鄉
試仍應停止其單開山西省之太原府忻州太谷
縣大同府汾州府孝義縣曲沃縣大甯縣河津縣岳
陽縣朔平府文水縣壽陽縣平陽府長子縣高平
縣澤州府隰州蒲縣絳州歸化城綏遠城河南省
之南陽府河內縣鄭州光州陳州府浙江省之衢
州府直隸省之北京順天府保定府永清縣天津
府順德府望都縣獲鹿縣新安縣通州武邑縣景
州灤平縣東三省之盛京甲子廠連山于慶街北
林子呼蘭城陝西省之甯羌州江西省之鄱陽縣

条约：在克林德遇害之处，树立与他身份相称的纪念牌坊。

The Protocol: A memorial archway shall be built at the site where Ketteler was killed, which should be appropriate for his position.

清政府耗银120万两，在克林德案发处——东单西总布胡同西口外，建起这座横跨崇文门内大街的克林德碑。这座由汉白玉和大理石打造的碑坊，高近8米，宽16米，蓝色琉璃瓦覆顶，规格极高。碑额、碑文尽如条约规定。克林德碑1903年1月竣工，几天后举行了落成典礼。各国公使、商人、驻军官兵均出席，20岁的载沣亲王代表光绪皇帝致祭。一年多前，这位亲王也曾代表皇帝赴德国向德皇威廉二世谢罪。

The Qing Government spent 1.2 million taels of silver in building this Ketteler Archway spanning Chongwenmen Avenue at western entrance to Xizongbu Alley in Dongdan, where Ketteler was killed. The archway was built of high standard white marble. Nearly 8 meters high and 16 meters wide, its roof was covered in blue glazed tiles. The inscriptions were made as stipulated by the treaty. The archway was completed in January 1903. Foreign envoys, merchants and garrisons all attended the inauguration ceremony and 20-year-old Prince Zai Feng delivered an elegiac address on behalf of Emperor Guangxu. The year before, the prince visited Germany to offer an apology to German Emperor William II on behalf of the Chinese emperor.

条约： 准许各国在北京以及北京到山海关的铁路沿线的12个战略要地派兵驻扎……

The Protocol: Allow the nations to garrison Beijing and the 12 places of strategic importance along the railway from Beijing to Shanhaiguan Pass...

这里曾是北京一户殷实人家的住宅，现在居住着日本驻军的高级军官。

This house, which had been the property of a well-off family in Beijing, became the residence of a high-ranking officer of the Japanese garrison.

在山海关驻军的一位日本军官。
An officer of the Japanese garrison in Shanhaiguan Pass

发展到后来，列强在中国许多战略要地也设炮驻军，这是驻威海的英国军营。
Later, the foreign powers deployed artillery and garrisoned troops in many other strategic locations. Pictured here is the British barracks in Weihai, Shandong.

东交民巷西口的大门和外国驻军士兵。
The gate at the western entrance to Dongjiaominxiang and foreign garrison soldiers

在使馆区进进出出的尽是戎装在身的各国军人。
Uniformed foreign soldiers coming and going in the legation quarters

条约： 赔款4亿5千万两白银。

The Protocol: Pay an indemnity of 450 million taels of silver.

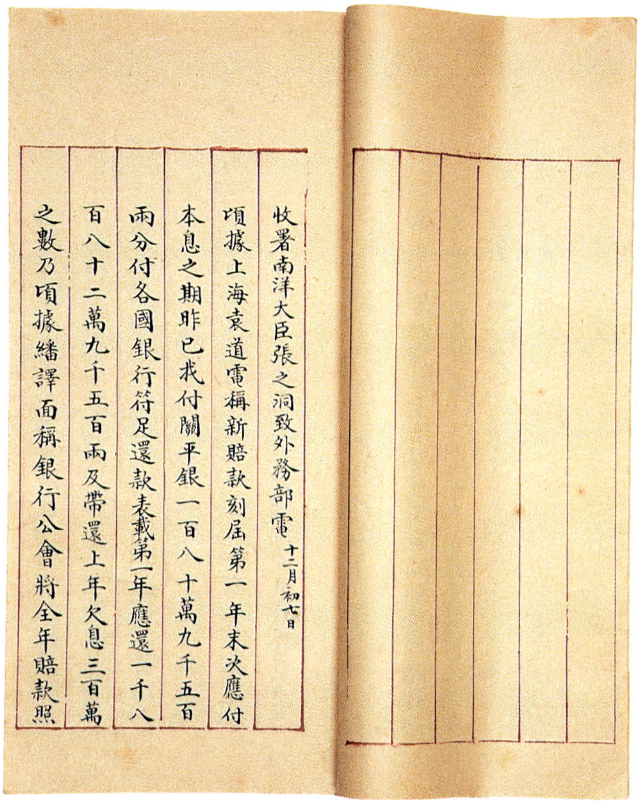

收署南洋大臣張之洞致外務部電 十二月初七日
頃據上海袁道電稱新賠款刻屆第一年末次應付
本息之期昨已找付關平銀一百八十萬九千五百
兩分付各國銀行符足還款表載第一年應還一千八
百八十二萬九千五百兩及帶還上年欠息三百萬
之數乃頃據繙譯面稱銀行公會將全年賠款照

湖广总督张之洞就筹款赔银事致电外务部。

Zhang Zhidong, Governor-General of Hubei and Hunan, telegraphed the Ministry of Foreign Affairs on raising funds to pay the indemnities.

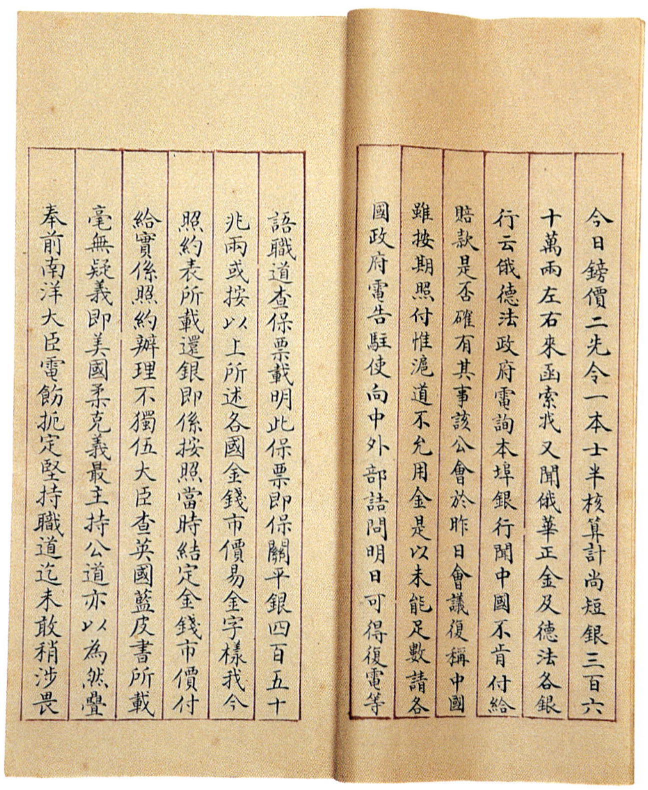

今日鎊價二先令一本士半核算計尚短銀三百六
十萬兩左右來函索找又聞俄華正金及德法各銀
行云俄德法政府電詢本埠銀行聞中國不肯付給
賠款是否確有其事該公會於昨日會議復稱中國
雖按期照付惟滬道不允用金是以未能足數請各
國政府電告駐使向中外部詰問明日可得復電等
語職道查保票載明此保票即保關平銀四百五十
兆兩或按以上所述各國金錢市價易金字樣我今
照約表所載還銀即係按照當時結定金錢市價付
給實係照約辦理不獨伍大臣查英國藍皮書所載
毫無疑義即美國柔克義最主持公道亦以為然疊
奉前南洋大臣電飭扼定堅持職道迄未敢稍涉畏

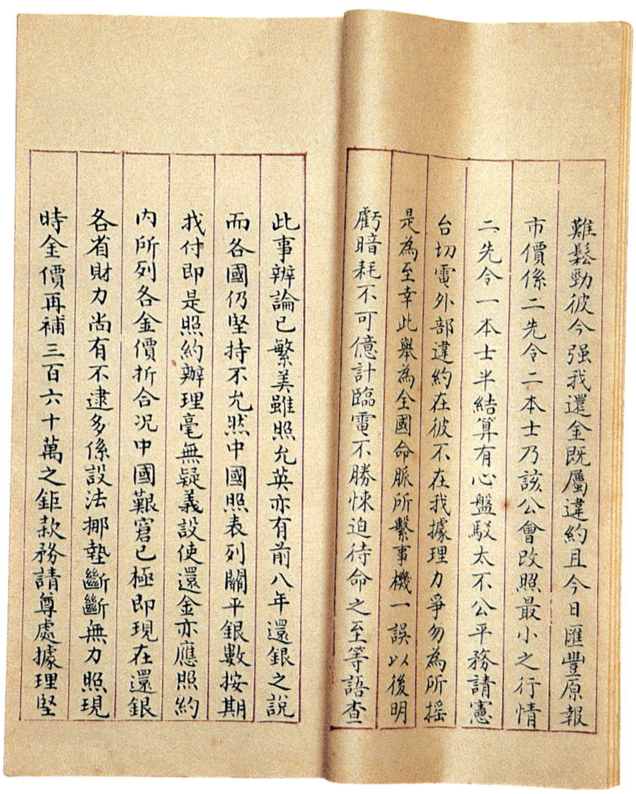

難鬆勁彼今强我還金既屬違約且今日匯豐原報
市價係二先令二本士乃該公會改照最小之行情
二先令一本士半結算有心盤駁太不公平務請憲
台切電外部違約在彼不在我據理力爭勿為所搖
是為至幸此舉為全國命脈所繫事機一誤以後明
虧暗耗不可億計臨電不勝悚迫待命之至等語查
此事辯論已繁美雖照允英亦有前八年還銀之說
而各國仍堅持不允然中國照表列關平銀數按期
找付即是照約辦理毫無疑義設使還金亦應照約
內所列各金價折合況中國艱窘已極即現在還銀
各省財力尚有不逮多係設法挪墊斷斷無力照現
時金價再補三百六十萬之鉅款務請尊處據理堅

条约： 改总理各国事务衙门为外务部，班列六部之首。

The Protocol: Change the Office for the Management of Business of All Foreign Countries into the Ministry of Foreign Affairs, which shall be ranked the first of the six ministries.

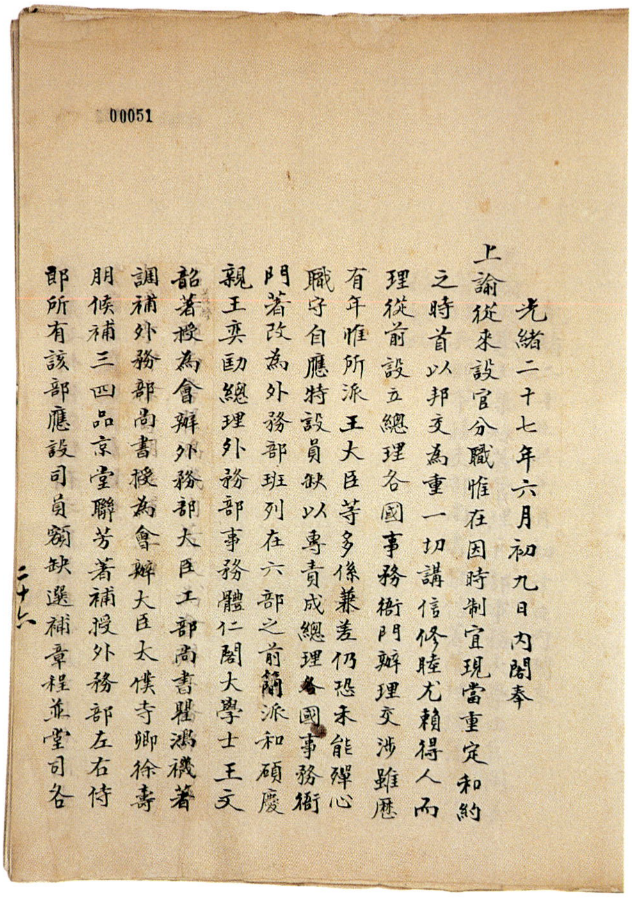

00051

光緒二十七年六月初九日內閣奉
上諭從來設官分職惟在因時制宜現當重定和約
之時首以邦交為重一切講信修睦尤賴得人而
理從前設立總理各國事務衙門辦理交涉雖歷
有年惟所派王大臣等多係兼差仍恐未能殫心
職守自應特設員缺以專責成總理各國事務衙
門著改為外務部班列在六部之前簡派和碩慶
親王奕劻總理外務部事務體仁閣大學士王文
韶著授為會辦外務部大臣工部尚書瞿鴻禨著
調補外務部尚書授為會辦大臣太僕寺卿徐壽
朋候補三四品京堂聯芳著補授外務部左右侍
郎所有該部應設司員額缺選補章程並堂司各

二十六

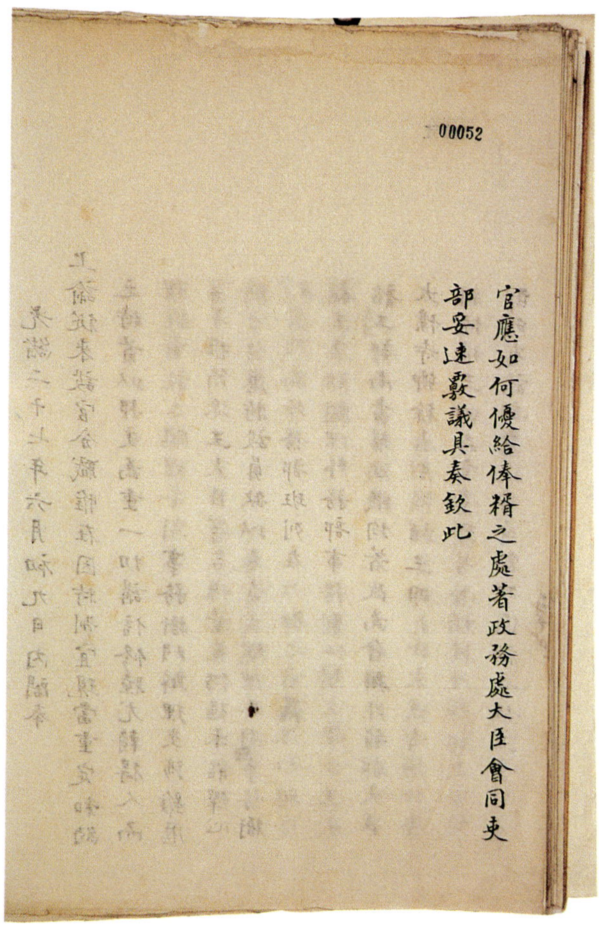

00052

官應如何優給俸糈之處著政務處大臣會同吏
部妥速覈議具奏欽此

关于改总理各国事务衙门为外务部的上谕。

The imperial edict on changing the Office for the Management of Business of All Foreign Countries into the Ministry of Foreign Affairs

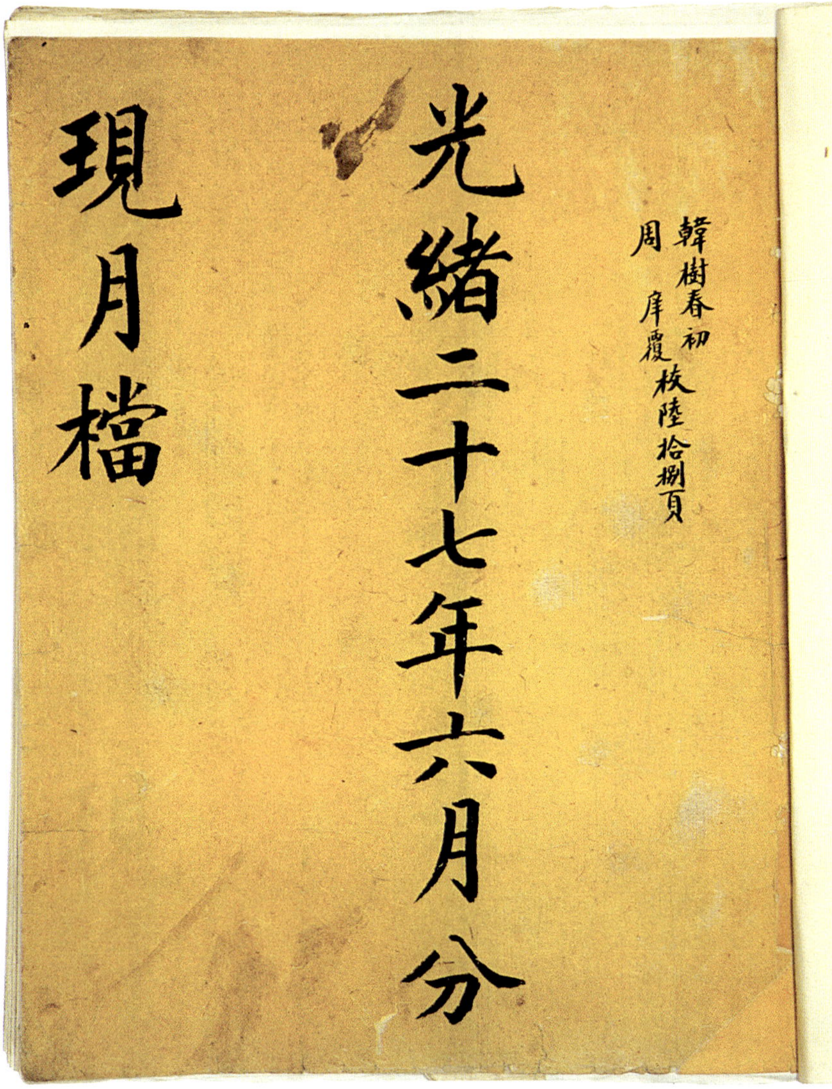

光緒二十七年六月分

現月檔

韓樹春
周庠霞 初校 陸拾捌頁

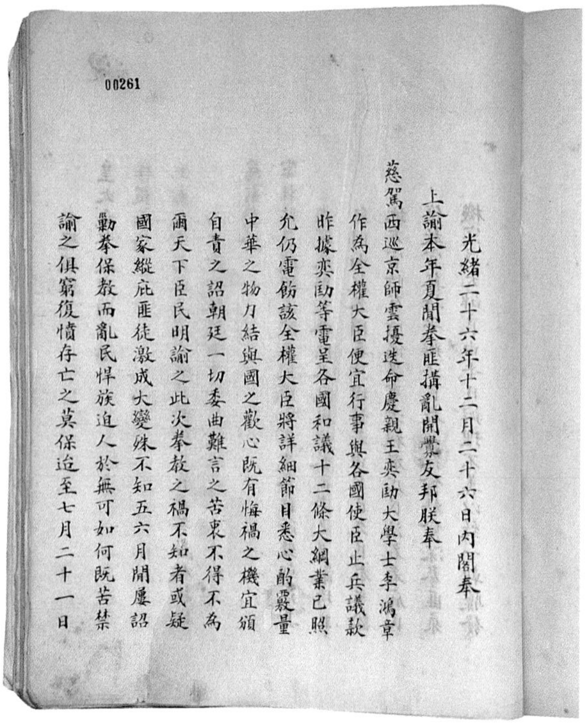

00261

光緒二十六年十二月二十六日內閣奉
上諭本年夏間拳匪搆亂開釁友邦朕奉
慈駕西巡京師雲擾迭命慶親王奕劻大學士李鴻章
作為全權大臣便宜行事與各國使臣止兵議款
昨據奕劻等電呈各國和議十二條大綱業已照
允仍電飭該全權大臣將詳細節目悉心酌覈量
中華之物力結與國之歡心既有悔禍之機宜頒
自責之詔朝廷一切委曲難言之苦衷不得不為
爾天下臣民明諭之此次拳教之禍不知者或疑
國家縱庇匪徒激成大變殊不知五六月間屢詔
勦拳保教而亂民悍族迫人於無可如何既苦禁
諭之俱窮復慚存亡之莫保迨至七月二十一日

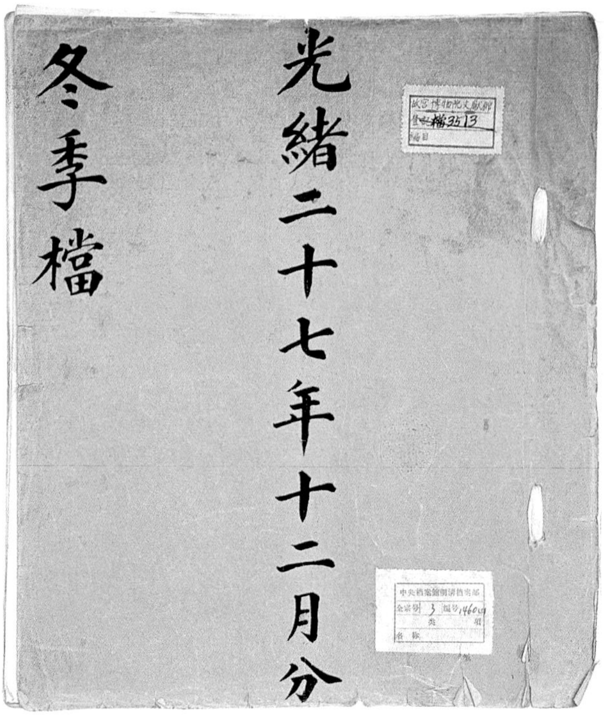

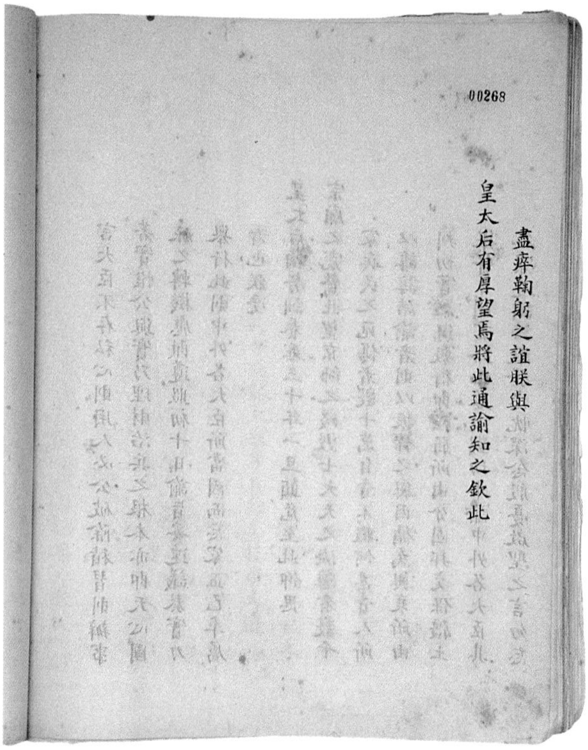

00268

盡瘁鞠躬之誼朕與
皇太后有厚望焉將此通諭知之欽此

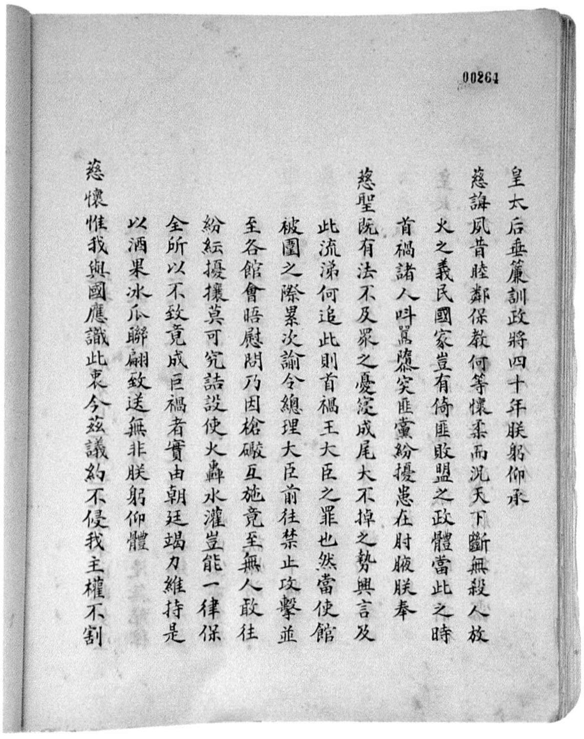

00264

皇太后垂簾訓政將四十年朕躬仰承
慈誨夙昔睦鄰保教何等懷柔而況天下斷無殺人放
火之義民國家豈有倚匪敗盟之政體當此之時
首禍諸人叫囂隳突匪黨紛擾患在肘腋朕奉
慈聖既有法不及眾之憂寖成尾大不掉之勢興言及
此流涕何追此則首禍王大臣之罪也然當使館
被圍之際累次諭令總理大臣前往禁止攻擊並
至各館會晤慰問乃因槍礮互施竟至無人敢往
紛紜擾攘莫可究詰設使火轟水灌豈能一律保
全所以不致竟成巨禍者實由朝廷竭力維持是
以酒果冰瓜聯翩致送無非朕躬仰體
慈懷惟我與國應識此衷今茲議約不侵我主權不割

有关“量中华之物力，结与国之欢心”的上谕。

The imperial edict on "exhausting the resources of China to please the Western nations"

清政府任奕劻（1836 – 1918）亲王为外务部首任尚书。从此，列强通过操纵外务部，谋取在华的各方面利益就更有隐蔽性。

The Qing Government appointed Prince Yi Kuang (1836-1918) as the first minister of the Ministry of Foreign Affairs. Through controlling the Ministry of Foreign Affairs, the foreign powers became more covert in seeking all kinds of benefits in China.

清政府应教会要求，依原样重建了被义和团烧毁的南堂教堂。

At the request of the church, the Qing Government rebuilt Nantang Cathedral (St. Mary of the Immaculate Conception Cathedral) as it was originally designed. The cathedral had been burnt down during the Boxer Uprising.

保定府拨库银为教案中死亡的外国教士立碑建亭。
A pavilion housing a tablet in memory of foreign missionaries who died in conflicts between non-Christian Chinese and foreign missionaries and Chinese converts, built with funds allocated by Baoding Prefecture

▼ 巨额赔款使中国进一步赤贫化。
The huge indemnities threw China further into abject poverty.

主宰中国政治舞台40余年的慈禧太后，实行政治、经济和文化专制。社会黑暗到了极点，清政府必然退出历史舞台。

Empress Dowager Cixi, who dominated China's political stage for more than 40 years, practiced political, economic and cultural autocracy. The extreme social darkness determined that the Qing Government must retire from the stage of history.

谁都想瓜分中国。英国报纸甚至登载了〝瓜分中国和平会章程〞，称〝所有中国土地既为万国管辖，任由万国通商。〞

谁都瓜分不了中国。赫德就承认〝义和团之运动，实由其爱国之心所发。〞他预言：〝中国如被瓜分，全国就将协同一致起来，反对参与瓜分的那几个外国统治者。〞历史证明了这一预言。

It was common among some foreign powers to want to carve up China. A British newspaper even published the "Articles of the Peace Council for Carving up China," claiming that "all nations should be able to conduct commercial activities in China, as all Chinese land is under the jurisdiction of the nations."

No one, however, was able to carve up China. Robert Hart admitted, "The Boxer Uprising was actually a result of patriotism." He predicted: "If China were carved up, the entire nation would unite to fight against the foreign rulers that participated in the carving." History has proved that he was right in this prediction.

本图册的编辑得到了徐玲、刘叶青、张晓东等专业人士和友人的热情帮助，特此致谢。

The compilation of this illustrated book has received the help of our friends Xu Ling, Liu Yeqing and Zhang Xiaodong. We hereby extend our thanks to them.

图书在版编目（CIP）数据:

外国人镜头中的八国联军:辛丑条约百年图志:汉英对照/《辛丑条约百年图志》编委会编. —北京: 外文出版社, 2001.9
ISBN 7-119-02914-2

Ⅰ.外… Ⅱ.辛… Ⅲ.八国联军—侵华—史料
Ⅳ.K256.706

中国版本图书馆CIP数据核字(2001)第061195号

外文出版社网址:
http: // www.flp.com.cn
外文出版社电子信箱:
info@flp.com.cn
sales@flp.com.cn

外国人镜头中的八国联军
—— 辛丑条约百年图志

出版发行: 外文出版社
印刷: 深圳市柯印纸制品印刷有限公司
开本: 787 × 1092 16开
字数: 20千字
印数: 1-6000册 印张: 15
版次: 2001年9月第一版第一次印刷
装别: 精
书号: ISBN 7-119-02914-2/Z·613(外)
85-CE-S24S
定价: ￥397元